Zen and the Beat Way

ZEN
and the
BEAT WAY

Alan Watts

—

CHARLES E. TUTTLE CO., INC.
Boston • Rutland, Vermont • Tokyo

First published in 1997 by
TUTTLE PUBLISHING,
an imprint of Periplus Editions (HK) Ltd.,
with editorial offices at
153 Milk Street, Boston, Massachusetts 02109.

The excerpt on page xviii-xix is from *The Windbell*, reprinted courtesy of Gordon
Onslo-Ford and the San Francisco Zen Center.

Library of Congress Cataloging-in-Publication Data

Watts, Alan, 1915-1973.
    Zen and the Beat way / Alan Watts.
        p. cm.
    Based on selections from Alan Watts's radio talks and
tape recordings; adapted and written by David Cellers
and Mark Watts.
    Cf. CIP pref.
     ISBN 0-8048-3117-3
    1. Zen Buddhism. I. Cellers, David. II. Watts, Mark.
III. Title.
BQ9266.W389 1997
294.3'927--dc21
                                     97-6843
                                       CIP

DISTRIBUTED IN THE UNITED
STATES BY
Charles E. Tuttle Co., Inc.
RR1 Box 231-5
North Clarendon, VT 05759
Tel: (800) 526-2778
Fax: (800) FAX-TUTL

IN JAPAN BY
Tuttle Shokai Ltd.
1-21-13, Seki
Tama-ku, Kawasaki-shi 214
Japan
Tel: (044) 833-0225
Fax: (044) 822-0413

AND IN SOUTHEAST ASIA BY
Berkeley Books Pte. Ltd.
5 Little Road #08-01
Singapore 536983
Tel: (65) 280-3320
Fax: (65) 280-6290

First Edition
05 04 03 02 01 00 99 98 97 1 3 5 7 9 10 8 6 4 2
Design by Kathryn Sky-Peck

Printed in the United States of America

Contents

Preface

德 *Zen and the Beat Way* is based upon selections from Alan Watts's early radio talks, many of which were first aired on the Pacifica Radio Network in the late fifties and early sixties, and sessions from two of his most compelling seminars in the mid-sixties. The original recordings have been adapted to the written page by David Cellers and Mark Watts.

Our first selection, "Introduction to the Way Beyond the West," was broadcast on KPFK in Los Angeles on November 6, 1959, and offered Southern Californians their first opportunity to listen to the popular Alan Watts series broadcast by KPFA in Berkeley during the previous six years. The second and third talks, "The Beat Way of Life" and "Consciousness and Concentration," were originally broadcast on KPFA on August 11 and 15, 1959, and shortly thereafter on KPFK. The radio series has continued on these stations in various forms for more than forty years. By the early sixties, tape recordings of public lectures, rather than radio talks, were being broadcast. Our fourth selection, "Zen and the Art of the Controlled Accident," was one such lecture, recorded in La Jolla, California, in early 1965, and "The Democratization of Buddhism" was recorded while on tour in Japan in 1963. The final selection, "Return to the Forest," was recorded in 1960 and includes a commentary on Joseph Campbell's work on the earliest counterculture traditions.

Robert Wilson: *What is Zen?*

Alan Watts: [Soft chuckling.]

Robert Wilson: *Would you care to enlarge on that?*

Alan Watts: [Loud laughing.]

Introduction

德 During a 1960 "impolite interview" for Paul Krassner's free-thought magazine *The Realist,* Robert Anton Wilson asked Alan Watts what he thought about the Beat generation. Alan replied that the concept was "a journalistic invention, and having been invented and put on the market, many people bought it." Alan then began to reminisce about the real Beats:

> *Now, I remember the real, original Dharma Bums of the 1945–46 era—young veterans hitchhiking across the country and stopping every place there was a "sage" who knew something about Eastern philosophy. Some even went to Switzerland to speak to Jung, and many came to see me at Northwestern University.*
>
> *They weren't interested in jazz or drugs or hot rods, I assure you. Many of them are still around, but very few of*

them in the Village or North Beach. They're on farms or in little communities they created themselves. They are out of the rat races of keeping up with the Joneses.

They are the substance of which the Beat generation is the shadow. [p.1]

By the late fifties the Beat movement was already a few incarnations removed from its origins, and clearly Alan Watts felt that Eastern thought had been inextricably tied to its genesis. And although it seems inevitable that many people will see the source of any social movement as its purest form, the phenomenon known as "the Beat way of life" was as much a reaction to the realities of mainstream American culture of that era as anything else. Politically, the 1950s were a dark period in American history. Cold-war paranoia found expression in McCarthyism and pitted the political process against free expression and the creative life. In the trials of Lenny Bruce and Lawrence Ferlinghetti, First Amendment rights came under attack. Today, freedom-of-speech questions are still judged according to their "redeeming social value," as they were in the trials of the fifties. The very act of being an artist or writer was in and of itself suspect, and the Beats reacted to the conservative climate with a well-balanced synthesis of anarchism and idealism. But underneath this colorful social chaos, it is important to remember that originally the Beat movement was a way of life with connections to Zen, and from Zen to Hinduism, and from Hinduism back to the dawn of human culture.

Recently I came across the following passage in Robert Lawlor's captivating book on Australian Aboriginal culture, *Voices of the First Day*:

> *The materialistic industrial societies are increasingly caught in a round-the-clock whirl in which people are trapped, day after day, in a breathless grind of facing deadlines, racing the clock between several jobs, and trying to raise children and rush through the household chores at the same time. Agriculture and industrialism, in reality, have created a glut of material goods and a great poverty of time. Most people have a way of life devoid of everything except maintaining and servicing their material existence 12 to 14 hours every day. In contrast, the Aborigines [spent] 12 to 14 hours a day in cultural pursuit.* [p. 65].

As Lawlor points out, "their traditional way of life provided more time for the artistic and spiritual development of the entire society. Dance, ritual, music—in short, culture— was the primary activity." The Aborigines passed the message of their ancestors down through a rich tradition of ritual storytelling, and their myths reflect the qualities of one of the oldest and most interesting surviving human cultures.

The Aboriginal view of creation is rooted in the idea of an original *dreamtime,* perhaps corresponding to a historical age, in which the conscious and unconscious aspects of mankind were unified "on the first day." Aboriginal ceremonies emphasize remembering that primal unity through ritual acts. According to their mythology, these ceremonies are visited by the Rainbow Serpent, described by Lawlor as "the original appearance of creative energy in the dreamtime." In the parallel Hindu myth of creation, the god Vishnu *dreams* the world into being while riding a great serpent in the cosmic ocean. In these Aboriginal and Hindu stories, one can see two similar tellings of the same essential myth.

Robert Lawlor shares his interest in the mythology of the Proto-Australoid peoples common to Australia and ancient India with Joseph Campbell, who was a great friend of Alan Watts and the posthumous editor of the works of Henrich Zimmer. Working from Zimmer's notes, Campbell wrote *The Philosophies of India,* which offered a tantalizing glimpse into the traditions from which Buddhism grew several thousand years ago. Sadhus of Dravidian ancestry still roam beyond the villages in India today, living much as the Aborigines did—without huts or clothes, in direct relationship and harmony with the physical and invisible worlds. As one becomes familiar with the religious psychologies in play, it is apparent that the unity of the human and the divine is embodied in the emergence of the individual from the dreaming of the god-head. This view is the essence of Hinduism and, ultimately, Buddhism. By contrast, the myths of creation adopted by the West place man on the earth beneath the celestial throne of an almighty Lord of the Heavens, to whom we owe not only our existence but also our complete obedience. Any aspiration or emulation of the deity is coupled with a fundamental separation from the deity.

Alan Watts's life can be described in part as a journey away from the limited conception of the divine he came to know in his early training for the priesthood. It was a journey that took him from London to California, through encounters with D. T. Suzuki, Joseph Campbell, and Gary Snyder, and from the Episcopal Church to the beatniks.

As a young man attending King's School in Canterbury, prior to entering the church as an Episcopal priest, Alan Watts was troubled by the image of God as a "cosmic tyrant." It just didn't make sense to him. Why would an infinitely wise ruler treat his subjects so harshly for their sins? God, in His infinite wisdom, had *created* such sinners, after all. Watts began to frequent the bookstores of London in search of a more plausible and comprehensive view of the divine. He read extensively, and within a few years he had followed his curiosity about such matters to the Buddhist Society in London, a philosophical organization guided by Christmas Humphrys. There he came into contact with the way of liberation known as Zen Buddhism. He was later to meet D. T. Suzuki there, and instead of going to Oxford, Watts became deeply involved in the activities of the Buddhist Society, including the publication of its journal, *The Middle Way*. After contributing several articles, he became its editor and wrote a regular column. These articles were soon followed by a pamphlet entitled *An Outline of Zen Buddhism* and then by a short book, *The Spirit of Zen*.

Alan Watts subsequently married Eleanor Everett, and they moved to America in 1938. In 1940, his book *The Meaning of Happiness* was published by Harper in New York. Much of the following decade was spent trying to fit in as a priest in the Episcopal Church. However, his early exposure to Zen Buddhism raised many difficult questions. In 1949, he wrote *The Supreme Identity* in a valiant attempt to reconcile Christianity with Buddhism and Vedanta, but in 1950 he left the church—and his wife—and soon married Dorothy DeWitt. Together they moved to a farmhouse in Millbrook, New York where later the same year he wrote *The Wisdom of Insecurity*.

On New Year's Eve in 1950, Alan and Dorothy invited Joseph Campbell and his wife, the accomplished dancer Jean Erdman, to dinner along with the avant-garde composer John Cage and Luisa Coomaraswami. The evening's conversations ranged from discussions of possible early transpacific voyages from Asia to America, to the latest innovations in music and dance, and then on to Joseph's experiences on the West Coast. The evening made quite an impression on Alan, who had already decided to move to San Francisco. On February 6, 1951, he and Dorothy departed for California to begin a new life.

Alan had accepted a teaching position offered by Fredric Spiegelberg at the Academy of Asian Studies in San Francisco. There he met poet Gary Snyder and Japanese artist Saburo Hasegawa. Both of them, in their own way, broadened his aesthetic appreciation of Zen and introduced him to various northern California artists and writers who were living what was known as the Beat way of life. When the academy moved to the Pacific Heights area of San Francisco, Spiegelberg asked Watts to give up his teaching position to serve as dean. The school was poorly organized, and the job proved to be quite stressful. On more than one occasion, Saburo invited Alan to stop by and enjoy a relaxing cup of tea in his office. The tea was Japanese green tea, offered in the style of the tea ceremony while participants were seated on the carpet. The tea ceremony eventually became quite popular in certain areas of San Francisco, due in part to the ongoing classes offered by Saburo's wife, Kiyoko.

Traditional brushstroke calligraphy also gained a

following in the Bay Area, due to the influence of both Saburo and Hodo Tobase. The well-known surrealistic painter Gordon Onslo-Ford became an avid student of Hasegawa's and later Tobase's, and both he and Alan fell in love with the paper, inks, and brushes used in calligraphy. Years later Gordon spoke of his first meeting with Saburo Hasegawa in an interview with Michael Wenger of the San Francisco Zen Center:

I should perhaps say how my interest in calligraphy started. There was a well-known Japanese painter called Sabro Hasegawa, who had been in New York, and had been a great friend of Franz Klein. Hasegawa was the editor of a calligraphy magazine in Japan, and he was interested in the liaison between the East and the West. He was scheduled to talk at the Asian Academy. Alan Watts, who was then the dean, telephoned me and told me that he was going to stay for a week, and would I look after him, and I agreed. So I went to Hasegawa's lecture, which was absolutely brilliant.

The next day I met Hasegawa and I took him for a walk in Muir Woods. We walked for two hours. Hasegawa was a man of tea. He was dressed in the most immaculate brown kimono. We walked for two hours, and he didn't say anything, and I didn't say anything. When we came back, I said to him, "Would you rather go and have some lunch at my house or would you rather go to my studio?" Hasegawa said "I would rather go to your studio." My studio was on board a ferry boat at that time. When we got on board, he looked around—he looked at the floor and he indicated that he would like to do some calligraphy. He started clearing the junk away and prepared a beautiful little place. Out of his sleeve he brought a wonderful stick of two-hundred-year-old ink and a beautiful roll of paper. And then he made a few characters. He made the character for infinity, and he made a one-two-three, which is a magnificent composition, as you know, because each line has to have a different weight and there is a different spacing between each line. That one-two-three was given to Alan Watts. Alan Watts said that D. T. Suzuki was coming, and that he would point it out to him, and Hasegawa said that he would be so happy if D. T. Suzuki would walk by it without noticing it.

The story about Hasegawa's calligraphy was one of Alan Watts's favorites and became familiar to listeners of a series of public radio talks Watts gave in Berkeley beginning in 1951. At the station he met program director Richard Moore, who years later at KQED in San Francisco would produce the Alan Watts television series *Eastern Wisdom and Modern Life.*

During this period Watts's occasional evening lectures at

the academy were well attended, and he soon became known for his comfortable speaking style and for the vitality of his philosophical inquires. His weekly radio show gained widespread popularity as he allowed his natural sense of humor to play into the context of his talks, and by the late fifties he was speaking quite playfully in such talks as "The Sense of Nonsense," "Unpreachable Religion," and "The Smell of Burnt Almonds."

In his autobiography he wrote about the academy and his own role in the formative period of the counterculture movement:

> The American Academy of Asian Studies was one of the principal roots of what later came to be known, in the early sixties, as the San Francisco Renaissance, of which one must say, like Saint Augustine when asked about the nature of time, "I know what it is, but when you ask me, I don't." . . . I know only that between, say, 1958 and 1970, a huge tide of spiritual energy in the form of poetry, music, philosophy, painting, religion, communications techniques in radio, television, and cinema, dancing, theater, and general life-style swept out of this city and its environs to affect America and the whole world, and that I have been intensely involved in it. It would be false modesty to say that I had little to do with it, and I am at once gratified and

ZEN AND THE BEAT WAY

horrified to see how a younger generation has both followed and caricatured my philosophy.

This philosophy included a blend of classical Eastern thought, insights and observations from his own mystical experiences, and a pragmatic view of man as an integral part of nature a full generation before ecological issues became popular. He felt, as he later told a group of college professors, that, in essence, mystical experience and ecological awareness were simply two ways of talking about the same experience, and he would refer to his topic by one or the other—depending upon his audience and inclination. At other times he presented an interpretation of religious experience revealing a Jungian influence, and at times he credited Buddha with being the world's first great psychotherapist for recognizing the psychological trap inherent in *any* view of a divine self. However, some of his most dramatic and controversial talks involved direct comparisons between psychotic and religious experiences. "If Christ were to show up today," he would ask, "would he be welcome in the church, or locked up in an insane asylum?" The local Beats enjoyed his irreverent expositions immensely, and Watts participated in evening coffeehouse discussions running into the early-morning hours, and in wild poetry readings where he recited interpretations of British nonsense poems.

In 1953 Watts—now the father of two young children—moved from the San Francisco peninsula to the hills of Marin County just north of the Golden Gate Bridge. Here Gary Snyder's practical and scholarly interest in Zen was a continuing source of inspiration for Alan. When Robert Anton Wilson asked Alan about Gary Snyder during his interview for *The Realist,* Alan replied, "He's a true Dharma Bum, a man of complete integrity. He's just the way Kerouac describes him in *The Dharma Bums*—little, wiry, bearded, Oriental-looking, always dressed in clothes that are old and patchy but scrupulously clean. I don't practice Zen the way he does, but there are many ways of doing it. I think very highly of Gary." Alan was living with Dorothy and their growing clan of children in Homestead Valley, and Gary was living in a cottage on a nearby hill that was called alternatively *Marin-an,* or "the horse forest hermitage." Beat poets Jack Kerouac and Allen Ginsberg were in town in those days, and they came to visit Gary, and naturally Alan became involved in their goings-on. One such affair was a famous party (recorded in *The Dharma Bums*) thrown by Locke McCorkle, who had a house down at the bottom of the hill below Gary's cottage. At the party, Kerouac, McCorkle, and Ginsberg all ended up running around naked, while Alan sat with old friends from Chicago dressed in their business suits.

However, the most significant aspect of the scene for Alan

was not the parties but Gary's little cottage on the hill. As he later recalled:

Gary had figured out—really and truly—how to live the simple life. Everyone complained about beatniks being dirty, and having filthy pads, but here Gary had this sweet, clean, neat little place. And he explained to me how to get by on practically no money—where to go for second-day vegetables, how to get certain kinds of grains, how to use the Goodwill, and so on. He had a very nice place, and I felt that although I was trying to be involved in respectable public affairs because I had children to support, that the very existence of Gary's place gave the universe a little bit of stability.

Shortly after the famous party, Gary went off to Japan to begin "a real Zen study." For a time Alan continued his involvement in the San Francisco Beat scene and in 1959 wrote *Beat Zen, Square Zen, and Zen*, which eventually earned him the somewhat undeserved reputation as "father of the hippies." However, his 1956 classic, *The Way of Zen*, had become a bestseller, and while others appreciated the Beat trend for its purity as a literary movement, Alan became less interested in the Beat movement than in the assimilation of Oriental culture into Western society. He whimsically predicted that within a few years Asia would become covered with superhighways and neon-lit hamburger and hot dog stands, and that at the same time frustrated Tibetan lamas would be studying Buddhism at the University of Chicago.

Alan's second marriage did not survive the wayward influences of the Beat movement, but he spent the rest of his life speaking and writing—humorously and with insight—about Taoist, Buddhist, and Hindu traditions. In his works he always expressed a particular affinity for what I think of as the earliest "beatniks": the Eastern wandering sages and masters who went "beyond the pale" and returned to the forest to regain the original state of being and to experience life as it was "on the first day" and as it is, underneath all our planning and thinking, even now.

CHAPTER ONE

Introduction to the Way Beyond the West

德 A little over six years ago [1953], I began a series of radio programs that have been running ever since under the general title *Way Beyond the West*. I think I may as well give you a short explanation of that title. It obviously has a double meaning. The first is geographical. The West Coast of the United States faces Asia across the Pacific. The Asian world is therefore literally way beyond the West. The second reason for choosing this title is that the English word *way* is perhaps the nearest translation that we can make to the Chinese word *tao*. It is usually pronounced "dow." The Tao means many things. Primarily, it means the way of nature, the process of the universe. But it also means a way of life, a way of living in accordance with that process. For example, in Japan there are many crafts and arts, and even sports, that have been influenced by Eastern philosophy and are called "ways." You all know the word *judo*. *Ju* means "gentle," *do* is the Japanese way of pronouncing *tao*.

Therefore, judo is the gentle way. Similarly, the Japanese also speak of fencing as *kendo*, the way of the sword. They speak of the tea ceremony sometimes as *chado*, the way of tea. In Japanese culture there are all sorts of these *dos*, and they not only indicate the technique or mastery of the technique of performing the given art but also imply that the art involves a way of life. Indeed, in almost the ancient Western medieval sense, every Japanese art is a mystery. One used to speak, you see, of the mystery of being a goldsmith, the mystery of being a stonemason, the mystery of being a carpenter. Today that probably strikes us as extraordinarily peculiar terminology. But the meaning of it was that every man's vocation in life—what the Indians call *svadharma*, which means approximately one's own function, one's own calling—is also a way of initiation into the mystery of life. It has a sort of religious function. So then, the "way" in this title, *Way Beyond the West*, is the way of deeper understanding, or something like that. But why do I say that this way of deeper understanding is beyond the West? The answer, I think, is that we have lost the idea that our occupations are vocations. Not everybody has. But to a very large degree, our idea of an occupation is that it is a way of making money. We make a very, very destructive division between work and play. We spend eight hours, or whatever it may be, at work in order to earn the money to enjoy ourselves in the other eight hours. And that is a perfectly ridiculous way of living. It is much better to be very poor indeed than to do something so stupid as boring ourselves and wasting ourselves for eight hours in order to be able to enjoy ourselves the other eight hours. The result of this fantastic division between work and play is that work becomes drudgery, and play becomes empty. When we say that our occupation should also be our vocation, we are speaking of a conception of life within which work and play should be identical.

It is interesting that Hindus, when they speak of the creation of the universe, do not call it the work of God, they call it the play of God, the *Vishnu-lila*, *lila* meaning "play." And they look upon the whole manifestation of all the universes as a play, as a sport, as a kind of dance—*lila* perhaps being somewhat related to our word *lilt*. We in the West have tended to lose the idea of our work, our profession, as being a way, a tao. Furthermore, our religions tend very much to lose sight of themselves as being a tao, or way. To a very large extent, Christianity, in what we might call its standard brand forms, does not quite fulfill the function that Buddhism and Vedanta, which is the central doctrine of Hinduism and Taoism, fulfill in Asian society.

Now, mind you, these ways I am talking about in Asia are not followed by an enormous number of people, except in a kind of nominal, superficial way. And I am not trying to make any vast comparisons between Asian society and Western society or to say that the total Asian way of life is superior to

ours. I do not think it is, but I do not think it is necessarily infe-
rior, either; it is just different. But the fact remains that there is
an aspect of Asian religion and philosophy that is very subdued
in Western religion and philosophy, so that you might say that
the Way, in the sense of the Chinese Tao, does not quite exist in
the West, in any recognizable form. It does exist, yes. It exists
unofficially, it exists occasionally, but it is never clearly recog-
nized. So, therefore, I want to devote some time now to going
quite thoroughly into what these Eastern Ways are.

Now, when we are first introduced to such subjects as
Buddhism or Vedanta or Taoism or Confucianism, we usually
encounter them as some form of religion. We may have read
books on comparative religion in which these phenomena are
classified with Judaism, Christianity, Islam, and so on. But this
is really very misleading. It is as misleading as if you were to get
a textbook on botany, on flowers, and suddenly came across a
few chapters on birds. You would think this was a rather odd
classification. Well, if you know anything much about these
forms of Asian spirituality, you get the same kind of a funny
shock when you see them classified along with such things as
Christianity or Judaism. This is not to say that they are superior
to Christianity and Judaism; they are simply different. They
have different functions. And when we classify them all as various forms of religion, then a discussion arises as to which is the
best one for everybody or the best for you or me. But I think the

difference is much more subtle than that. And I can best approach this difference by saying that in the West we have primarily three forms of wisdom—religious, philosophical and scientific—but a way in the Asian sense is none of these.

First of all, the word *religion* comes from the Latin root *religare*, which means "a rule of life." *Religare* means "to bind, to bind oneself to something." We say of a person who has become a monk or a nun that he or she has gone into religion, which means that they have accepted a rule of life involving certain vows of poverty, chastity, and obedience, and other things as well. And the rule of life that constitutes a religion seems to me to consist of a creed, first of all, which is a system of revealed ideas about man and the universe and God, which one believes in and puts one's faith in.

The great Asian ways that I am speaking of do not, strictly speaking, have any creeds. They do not involve belief. That is to say, they do not involve committing oneself to certain positive opinions about life. Almost to the contrary, they abandon ideas and opinions because what they are concerned with is not ideas, not theories, but experience; experience in the sense almost of sensuousness, for instance, as they say, you drink water and know for yourself that it is cold. So, it is knowledge rather than faith that they are concerned with. Faith, as I am using it here, refers to a system of belief rather than a sense of trust. Very often it seems to me that faith and belief could be opposed. Belief comes from the Anglo-Saxon root *lief,* which means "to wish." Belief is the fervent hope that certain things are true. Whereas I rather feel that faith is an openness of attitude, a readiness to accept the truth, whatever it may turn out to be. It is a commitment of oneself to life, to the universe, to one's own nature as it is, in the realization that we really have no alternative. When you get into the water to swim, you have to trust yourself to the water. If you tighten your muscles and cling to the water, you will sink.

It seems to me that a religion, in addition to having a creed, also has a code. That is to say, it has a system of ethical and moral principles that one abides by because they are revealed as expressing, in the field of human conduct, the nature and will of the divine. And these Eastern ways do not have a code in that sense. One often speaks of the moral code of Buddhism, but this is a little inexact. What is involved here is not any attempt to make man accord with the nature of God or the will of God, but rather to suggest certain principles of action that are conducive to the discovery of the experience lying at the heart and the root of Buddhism. In addition to a creed and an ethical code, the idea of religion seems to me also to include a cult, a system of symbols and rites and ceremonials that in a certain way symbolically integrate the worshiper with the Godhead. And although there are rites and forms in Buddhism and Hinduism, not so much of worship but of thanksgiving, they are not regarded as very essential. They are not essential in the same way, for example, that Catholicism regards the rite of the mass as essential. So, all in all, it would be difficult to say that Buddhism and Vedanta and Taoism are religions, if Christianity or Judaism defines what we mean by *religion*. I do not want to dogmatize about the meaning of this word, but this is the way I use it, to mean a rule of life that has as its function the integration of a community, the binding together of a community. When one becomes a Jew, when one becomes a Christian, what one essentially does is join a society. We join a community. And in a way, we could say the function of a religion is what is called in Sanskrit *loca san hai,* which means the upholding of the world, the upholding of the order of the community. Every community must have rules. We must have rules of language in order to be able to communicate with one another. We must agree that we are going to use the noise *cloud* when referring to those things in the sky, instead of *yun,* the noise the Chinese use for them. We say "cloud"; they say "yun." Which is the right noise? It does not matter so long as the community in question agrees. This is what we call a *convention.* We agree by convention to drive on the right side of the road. So, every community needs a system of conventions, and it seems to me that what religion originally provided was, as it were, a divinely sanctioned system of conventions under which the community lives.

Now, the function of Buddhism is not so much the creation of a community. The function of Confucianism is to create a community, to lay down rules and conventions for a community. Parts of Hinduism, what one calls the caste system or the Laws of Manu, are concerned with laying down the rules for a community. But Vedanta and Buddhism and Taoism have almost the opposite function, which is not to enforce the conventional rules but to liberate the mind from enchantment by social convention. This is not a revolution against social convention, it is a perception that the rules of society are only conventions and that, in other words, the rules of a society, of language, of thought, of conduct, are not identical with the laws of God—or if you prefer, the laws of nature, the processes of nature.

We know perfectly well, for example, that it is very convenient to agree upon lines of latitude and longitude so that we can establish positions on the face of the globe. But we jolly well know that when we cross the equator we are not going to trip over a wire; it is an imaginary line, it is not really there.

Well, in the same way, all sorts of things that we believe to be real—time, past and future, for instance—exist only conventionally. A person who lives for the future, who (like most of us) makes his happiness dependent upon what is coming in the future, is living within an illusion. He or she has confused a convention with a reality. As even our own proverb says "Tomorrow never comes."

One of the functions of a way of the Tao is to deliver human beings from what Whitehead called "the fallacy of misplaced concreteness"; from confusing convention with reality; from confusing the laws of society with the actualities of the concrete, real world. It is in this sense, then, that the Tao is a way of liberation from social convention.

Now, just as these ways are not religion, so are they not philosophy, in the Western sense of the word. Philosophy, as we know it academically in the West, consists of a primarily verbal activity: constructing ideas and speculating about man and life, about the nature of knowledge and the nature of being, and about the problems of ethics and aesthetics. And, of course, more recently modern analytical philosophy has concerned itself with the logical structure of ideas. It is fundamentally, we might say, antimetaphysical because it feels that a great many metaphysical ideas are simply the result of linguistic and logical confusions. But by and large, you see, philosophy is concerned with ideas and their expression in words—that is to say, with the building up of a purely intellectual structure. That is philosophy as we know it in the West: the academic kind of philosophy.

Here again, Eastern ways are not philosophy. Just as they are not concerned with beliefs, they are also not concerned with intellectual theories, except in a purely secondary way. The heart of Buddhism and Vedanta is a transformation of man's consciousness, something that we in the West might call "mystical experience."

I do not like the word *mystical,* because it often has very, very weird connotations. One might speak more strictly of metaphysical experience; but even here, I do not really like that phrase, either. I prefer something much more solid. The experience the Buddhists are concerned with, for instance, is very concrete. It is not anything abstract. Abstractions belong to the realm of theory. Instead, the transformation of consciousness that the Buddhists talk about is almost, you might say, a new way of using one's senses. And thus it is not at all wishy-washy; it is not at all misty—if the word *mysticism* has any associations with mist.

And just as the Tao is not religion or philosophy, it is also not quite science—although in some respects it is very close to science.

Scientists are very often men of real faith. An honest scientist is a person who wants to know what this world really is. They do not want to be bamboozled by theories and hypotheses; they want to face the facts.

But the great interest of science, it seems to me, is not actually the facts or the concrete world but the representation of the concrete world in terms of certain codes—the codes of numbers, of algebraic symbols, or of formulae of various kinds—by which the scientist represents the world. These codes are rather like a photograph of a person's face reproduced in a newspaper. Look closely at a newspaper reproduction of a person's face and you will see that it is composed of a lot of little dots. Well, you jolly well know that a person's face is not really made out of a lot of little dots, even if you can arrange little dots on paper in such a way that they will look like a face. In other words, these dots merely re-present the face in terms of dots. Similarly, science re-presents human experiences, gained through our senses and through scientific instruments, in terms of linear symbols, in order to predict the future course of events. In other words, the practical function of science is prediction, and by such means the human control of the environment.

It is at this point that a way of liberation departs from what we mean by science because the focus of its interest is not so much on the future, on what will happen, but on the present. Because, after all, if we open our eyes and do not let our mind interfere too much with what we are actually perceiving, it is surely clear that we live only in the present. It is always *now*. So, this may seem tautological and redundant. It may seem to be something that everybody knows. But it really is not. Most of us judge the duration of the present by the little lines on our watches that mark off the seconds. They are just as thin as they can be. Therefore, the present is no time at all. And so, you see, we in the West all get the feeling that we have no time. Everybody says, "I am so busy. I have no time for this or that or the other thing." This feeling arises because we are beguiled by time. We are beguiled by watches. We really believe that the present lasts only a split second. All these Eastern ways are concerned with waking up, with coming to be dehypnotized—in the sense that every culture hypnotizes us. Waking up is what Buddhism means by *bodhi*, or enlightenment. *Buddha* is a title; it means "the man who woke up" or "the awakened one." But the moment a child comes into the world, people start talking or suggesting to it, and they very soon persuade it that the world is in fact the way they and their particular culture view it. Well, as the song says, it ain't necessarily so. The concept of time is one of the great ways in which we are fooled. We believe that the past and the future are, as it were, more solid and of longer duration than the present. In other words, we live in a sort of hourglass with a big bulb at one end (the past) and a big bulb at the other end (the future); we are at the little neck in between, and we have no time. Whereas when our vision becomes changed, we see that the truth of the matter is that we have, in fact, an enormous present in which we live and that the purely abstract borders of this present are the past and the future.

A coin has two faces, but they are merely surfaces; they are Euclidean and abstract; they have no thickness. The reality of the coin is the metal between the two surfaces. So, in somewhat the same way, the reality of time is the present lying between the past and the future, and the past and future are merely abstractions.

Now, although Eastern ways share something of the scientist's spirit of openness and nondogmatism, they are not sciences. They are not primarily concerned with predicting the future. That is not to say that they reject the future. They just do not care about it. One might put it this way: there is no point in caring about the future and making plans unless you are capable of living completely in the present, because when your plans mature and the future comes, if you cannot live in the present, there is no use you can make of the plans that have matured. You cannot enjoy what has happened if you cannot live in the present. You will always be looking over the shoulder of the event that has become present for something else still to come.

I have tried to show, by contrasting it with the three great forms of Western wisdom, what the Way beyond the West is all about. It exists for a minority in Asia, and I feel that in the present climate of Western science and philosophy, our great religious upheaval, and our discontent with our own traditions, it is enormously interesting and of great value to us. I am not—I must be very emphatic about this—a missionary for Zen Buddhism or Taoism trying to convert Western people to these things. On the contrary, I am trying to integrate their ideas with our own. American civilization is a syncretism of cultures of peoples, and this integration of Eastern and Western ideas is simply going to happen. And it is that integration that is the Way beyond the West.

CHAPTER TWO

The Beat Way of Life

 I am going to begin by quoting from a letter written by one friend of mine to another:

Never before this trip to the Bay Area have I seen so many people striving to get in tune with nature, to abandon themselves to the dictates of their muscles, to transcend their egos, to identify with the cosmic pond scum, to produce controlled accident—in which the accent invariably is an accident because these people know nothing of control—to build houses out of natural materials, and then to wash the boards with concrete so as to enhance the naturalness, etc. It is astonishing that anyone gets any work done at all.

I wonder why it is that the peculiar cluster of cultural phenomena that we call "the Beat way of life" arouses such antagonism. It is very difficult not to be involved in this kind of antagonism. People say to me, "You and you Taoist Zen types, what a mess you're making among the young people today, who don't have the hang of things yet. Supplying them with ideas from alien cultures in ways that are really completely subversive of the values that all right-thinking people support."

I remember not so long ago walking around Greenwich Village on one of the main streets, I forget which it was, where there were a lot of cafés and coffee shops and secondhand book-stores. It was about eight o'clock on a summer evening, and the street was full of people standing around talking. They weren't making any trouble, they were just standing there talking, but they were the strangest-looking bunch of people you ever saw, with beards and ponytails and weird getups. They just looked so terribly un-American. And there was a cop on duty, and I was watching him. You could see he was beginning to get the fidgets. Nobody was throwing rocks; nobody was making impolite remarks about him. They were just talking. But suddenly he couldn't contain himself any longer, and he said, "Hey, break it up there, move along, move along, get out of here." And the crowd slowly started to shift and gather somewhere else.

I remember, too, an article that was written in the *Herald Examiner,* I think. I cannot remember the author's name; he was a man who died in a plane crash with Mike Todd. I remember his saying that the real Americans were the fine fellows who were working on the missiles at Cape Canaveral and that all the poets, the painters, the sensation-seekers, and jazz fiends of San Francisco were just a bunch of poor sick little spoiled brats. And he was able to say this with a real convincing kind of tough-guy righteousness. Wherever there's a phenomenon like the Beats, the people who like to be righteously indignant about something have a perfectly wonderful opportunity to indulge themselves. It's like a good outbreak of sin. That's always so reassuring to the preacher because then he can get up in his pulpit and really lay down the law.

Now, of course, as everybody knows, there are two distinct kinds of people involved in this Beat phenomenon. I say "distinct" simply for purposes of discussion, because in nature you never find two distinct kinds of anything. They wash into one another like the bands in a rainbow. But broadly speaking, part of what is called the Beat movement is simply this: a lot of young people have in recent years come to the conclusion that the thing to do in life is pursue what used to be called their own vocation or calling, come what may, even if it is not rewarding economically or in terms of status.

I was talking just recently to a woman who is approaching middle age, I'd guess, who had spent most of her life doing something she did not want to do. She worked in some kind of a profession, and she hated it. She was pretty good at what she did, she had made a fair living, but she just hated doing it. It was not real, was not her. And so I said to her, "Well, then, what do you really want to do?" And she answered, "You know, I really want to fish."

Now, if you tell somebody who's deeply involved in the economic rat race that what you really want to do is fish, they're usually going to say, "Good heavens, everybody would like to go off for a weekend and fish. That's play. But if you're going to fish for a living, you know, that's not playing anymore, that's a tough life." But what I said to her was, "Well, why don't you just do it?" And she said, "You know, maybe I could. Maybe I could invest in one of those boats that take tourists out fishing off Santa Barbara. But what would my friends in my profession say?" So I said, "Well, go ahead and do it. Because you will not lose any real friends by changing your status in that way. What on earth is the point of knocking yourself out eight hours a day doing something you do not like, that you have no real gift for, just to spend the rest of your time in a hectic pursuit of fun?" Nobody really does anything well unless they can put their whole heart into it. Therefore, a job that you are doing just to keep body and soul together, that you do not respect, is always something you will not do as well as you might. And so a lot of young men have come to the realization that instead of making money to live some other time—that is, after hours, or when they retire and are older—they have decided that they should do what they really want to do now, come what may, even if it means living in a shack. And since there are always women who feel the same way, or else will go along with a man who really knows where he is going, these men also have wives and families. They don't have to become celibate hermits. And so such people are painting because they know that is what they really want to do, or some of them are carpenters or unofficial architects or writers or poets. A lot of these people will work as carpenters or loggers or seamen, or something of that kind, until they earn enough money to knock off for a few months and do what they really want to do.

This is one aspect of what has come to be called the Beat movement. It is what I would call the productive aspect. These people, as far as I can see, do not congregate in the notorious centers of the movement, like the North Beach in San Francisco or Greenwich Village, or Venice, California. Very often they live in a sort of exurbia, living a country kind of life.

On the other hand, there are people who are what I would call imitators of this attitude. And these are, of course, the people about whom it is so very easy to get angry.

We can say of them that they are just playing a role; they are merely imitators of what is actually a new way of life and a new force artistically. They are just pretenders. They have the beards, the blue jeans, the jazz records, the marijuana. But they don't do anything. They just play at being Beats. They lie around all the time and are completely unproductive. They are weak people, parasites, exploiting a new cult.

Oh, yes, it is awfully easy to say that. They expose them-selves to this kind of criticism, and it is real fun to throw bricks at them. But whenever we get angry about a person or a group of people, it is always instructive to look into our own uncon-scious situation and find out why we hate them so much or why we feel threatened enough by their way of life to get mad at them. Well, of course, the extreme beatnik way of life is the direct opposite of everything that every solid American citizen is supposed to be. It is an unproductive life. It is a lazy life, without ambition, and a rejection of the whole idea of being a good consumer.

Now, I think Freud and Jung had a very great insight when they pointed out that the constellation of motives in the uncon-scious mind is always likely to be the opposite of those that exist in the conscious mind, so that together they form a kind of com-pensatory relationship between what we are consciously and what we are unconsciously. Now, I think this can be carried too far. It can impose upon human beings a too logical, too mechan-ical, dualistic theory of the emotions. But, nevertheless, there is truth in it. Therefore, when a good American male gets angry because he thinks a fellow is a homosexual, it is perfectly clear that he is angry because he feels threatened by unconscious doubts about his own heterosexuality. In the same way, when solid citizens get angry when confronted by people simply doing what they want to do—or maybe just putting on an act,

ZEN AND THE BEAT WAY

just playing a role because it is *de rigueur*—doesn't it mean that in our heart of hearts we feel that these people constitute a threat? Doesn't it mean we feel the Beats are suggesting that the way of life we solid citizens are pursuing is not worth it, that there is something wrong with it?

We criticize people like this for being unproductive because we believe in productivity. As Wendell Willkie used to say in his election speeches back in 1940, "Only the productive can be strong, and only the strong can be free." But if we think about that statement, we begin to realize that it isn't true. It is perhaps true that only the productive can be strong, but when we go on to say that only the strong can be free, we are really saying that freedom can be maintained only by force, by strength. It is like a rather similar saying, that the price of freedom is eternal vigilance. And that statement, when we analyze what it is actually saying, means that only a police state can guarantee democracy because that is what eternal vigilance is: eternal vigilantes. In other words, according to this philosophy, freedom must be based on a kind of mutual mistrust, with everybody watching everybody else to see that no one oversteps the limits. In fact, that leads not to freedom but to everybody being his brother's policeman; everybody snooping after somebody else to be sure no one does anything wrong, like those police forces that take it upon themselves to prevent crime rather than simply to apprehend the criminal after the crime has occurred. Well, it is all very laudable theoretically. What it means in reality, though, is everybody snooping and making a nuisance of themselves and suspecting everybody else.

You cannot take a walk in Beverly Hills without being stopped by the police—because people down there do not walk, they drive. Therefore, if you are walking, you must be some kind of a suspicious character. It is not true, in other words, that freedom depends on that kind of strength. Freedom depends on the ability of people to trust one another. If a society is incapable of that kind of trust, it is also incapable of freedom.

But if one really believes that only productivity can create strength—that a human being, in other words, has to justify himself or herself by producing something—then maybe the psychoanalysts are right, and everything does go back to toilet training and mother's saying, "Have you produced today, have you done your duty?" I don't know. It seems to me in a way more likely that this emphasis on productivity goes back to the great age of scarcity, when if people did not work, they didn't have anything to eat. We do not have that situation today. In fact, we are working hard against it. Although our psychology hasn't kept pace with the idea, we are deliberately creating an economy in which machines do our work for us, and an abundance of food is produced. So we have got to learn how to loaf.

All right. The Beats are simply loafing. But many solid citizens are productive only in a limited sense. They are involved in the system of production only so they can go back home after work and sit passively and watch television. And I do not know whether it is better to watch the average television show or to lie on your back in some pad, smoking marijuana and listening to jazz. What is the difference? It is only that one choice is an overt and obvious divergence from the social norm, and the other is not. But, you see, here is the problem. Unless human beings can accustom themselves to the idea of being in a state of leisure, they are not going to be able to adapt themselves to the economy that they themselves are creating. If one has to go on producing for the sake of producing, that is like an airplane in flight. It can never hover. It must go on doing what it is doing, or collapse. In a culture where everybody has to keep producing, even though plenty is produced already, all kinds of propaganda have to be generated to get people to buy up the surplus production. But in order to find the means to buy it, they have got to create surplus production. Well, this is a vicious circle of major dimensions. And although we may not like, aesthetically or morally, the role that the more irresponsible beatniks are playing, it is a role that in a way emerges almost of necessity in our particular kind of civilization. In other words, people who are going to be nonproductive, who are going to be fundamentally lazy, are going to idealize a life of a certain kind of poverty. And they are going to explore realms of experience that solid citizens have not explored and are indeed afraid to explore—the inner world, the world of imagination and fantasy and the unconscious. We are afraid to explore the unconscious, even though it is what I might call the real "New Frontier." We have already explored the geographical frontiers of this earth, and it is going to take us a terribly long time to get out into the outer reaches of the solar system, but the frontier of the inner world is there waiting for us. But it is frightening; it is unknown.

Now, admittedly, a great many people who are involved in this "sensation-seeking way of life" may indeed be weak. They may indeed be nothing more than caricatures of something else that is real and has a purpose. Nevertheless, when has there ever been an artistic movement, a spiritual movement, a political movement, or a literary movement that did not have hangers-on, caricatures of the thing, who made themselves and the movement vulnerable to all kinds of ridicule? There have always been hangers-on. There are always going to be people who will imitate real things in a superficial manner. And it is so easy to focus on the superficial imitators, and judge the whole movement by them. This is always done by anybody who wants to laugh at something. If you want to attack Christianity or if you want to attack Buddhism, you always pick on its worst manifestations and attack them. And so it is with the situation today. But as the proverb says, Where there is smoke, there is fire. Superficial imitators are like smoke. Where you see smoke, look out for the fire. Where you find a weak caricature, you should always look beneath it to see what is being imitated. If there is all this hullabaloo today about, as my friend said in his letter, getting in tune with nature, transcending the ego, identifying with the cosmic pond scum, producing controlled accidents, and so on, it merely means that underneath this caricature there is enough going on that hangers-on think they can gain some status for themselves by copying it. To the extent that the thing being copied is real, the copy cannot do the real thing any serious harm. As I was saying earlier, if you set out to do what you really want to do, you may lose a lot of friends but you will not lose a single friend who is worth having. In the same way, a movement like the Beat way of life, for instance, or one interested in Oriental philosophy may be made vulnerable to ridicule because of its hangers-on, but they will not do it any real harm, and they will not lose it any friends worth having.

CHAPTER THREE

Consciousness and Concentration

 I want to start with two quotations. The first is from Freud's *Civilization and Its Discontents*.

> *Originally, the ego includes everything; later it detaches itself from the external world. The ego feeling we are aware of now is thus only a shrunken vestige of a far more extensive feeling, a feeling which embraced the universe and expressed an inseparable connection of the ego with the external world.*

So much for Freud. The second is by Gardner Murphy, professor of psychology at Columbia University, from his book *Personality*.

> *If, moreover, we are serious about understanding all we can of personality, its integration and disintegration, we must understand the meaning of depersonalization, those*

experiences in which individual self-awareness is abrogated and the individual melts into an awareness which is no longer anchored upon self hood. Such experiences are described by Hinduism in terms of the ultimate unification of the individual with the Atman, the super individual cosmic entity which transcends both selfhood and materiality. Some men desire such experiences, others dread them. Our problem here is not their desirability, but the light they throw on the relativity of our present-day psychology of personality. Personality, ordered largely with reference to self-awareness, has until recently appeared to be the fundamental reality, but it must be seen against the background of a wide variety of cross-cultural conditions, and of developmental disassociational and degenerative states in our own culture. Some other mode of personality configuration in which self-awareness is less emphasized, or even lacking, may prove to be the general or the fundamental.

I cite these two quotations just to suggest that it is not only so-called mystics and devotees of Oriental religions who feel that there is something a little wrong or unnatural about our ordinary way of feeling about ourselves and the surrounding world. The psychologist as well as the mystic may easily hit upon the idea that human beings are bedeviled by a fundamental twist of perception, a distortion of their whole feeling of life, which lies at the root of a large constellation of moral, psychological, and spiritual problems.

As you know, the detection and straightening out of this twist is the great preoccupation of Indian and Chinese philosophy. As Gardner Murphy says, they look toward a state of consciousness in which individual self-awareness is abrogated and the individual melts into an awareness that is no longer anchored upon selfhood.

This is not, however, to be understood as a kind of trance in which the individual is incapable of relating him- or herself to the practical affairs of everyday life. It is rather the perception of the same everyday world from a new standpoint, a standpoint from which the same facts and events have an entirely different sense.

To a considerable extent (though with some exceptions), the philosophers of India and China have looked upon this transformation of awareness as the fruit of an arduous course of spiritual and psychological discipline, a discipline so rigorous and prolonged that it puts such a transformation of awareness beyond the attainment of all but a few spiritual heroes extraordinarily gifted with courage and willpower.

In East and West alike, however, men are always looking for shortcuts or simplifications of these difficult tasks. Some of these shortcuts are perhaps no better than the phony correspondence courses that lure subscribers with promises of being able to amaze your friends after only six weeks' study of some marvelous, easy way of becoming a genius at the piano. Maybe the Oriental equivalent to this is the prayer wheel.

However, laziness is the mother of invention, as well as of self-deception. For time and time again we find that we have made a certain problem incredibly difficult for ourselves by failing to understand it clearly or by failing to find the right technique for handling it.

Think of the difficulty of doing complex multiplication or long division with Roman numerals or of moving heavy loads without wheels or of computing the movement of the planets before Copernicus's simplified view of the solar system.

As a naturally lazy person, I have always been intrigued with the possibility of simplifying this whole basic problem of changing man's awareness. So often in these talks I have minimized the role of effort and willpower and struggle in this task, thus earning the disdain of puritans and muscular religionists who do not realize that in many respects, laziness is as creative as brawn and vigor.

I suppose the trouble with these people is that they have basically an economic view of the spiritual life. For them, that life is subject to the laws of supply and demand. Whatever becomes common or usual must also become cheap. In this view, sages would turn into fools if they became as plentiful as fools.

I do not think that this economic analogy is at all proper. I would rather compare the kind of awareness I am thinking about to something like eyesight. Just about everyone has it, and yet to everyone it is incredibly precious. There may be a great deal of difference in value in what we do with our eyes, between looking at TV commercials and looking at great works of art, but in both cases we are aware of the marvel and the work of sight itself.

I would like, therefore, to talk about what is probably a very foolish notion of mine. I want to talk about it in a very tentative and experimental way, just as if I were thinking out loud.

It may be a symptom of my natural laziness and nothing more than that, yet it is one of my strongest intuitions—and has been for years—that it is basically a very simple matter for people to shift from what I will call the egocentric to the universal mode of awareness. I am quite sure that there are very difficult ways of doing it as well. In time past, people came upon these ways and embodied them in traditions that have been handed down to others. We easily assume that the way we learned to do something is the only way to learn it; therefore, the most tortuous mountain path is the only path if you learned no other.

For example, if you have watched Hindu dancing, you would have noticed the curious and fascinating gesture of moving the head from side to side so that it seems to float above the shoulders, detached from the neck. Now, you can spend months and almost sweat blood learning this trick unless someone points out that it comes quite naturally if you will simply hold up your arms and then try to touch your biceps with your ears. It is a little awkward at first, but very soon you get the hang of it, even though it's been described by experts as a strange dislocation of the neck that no Westerner can ever learn. It is the old story of the mysterious East, which is not really so mysterious after all. The apparent mystery is that Eastern teachers of any art, whether dancing or yoga, always tend to make you find out things for yourself, and you therefore often persist for ages on a completely wrong track.

The central difficulty of almost all forms of spiritual discipline is that they require prolonged and intense concentration, usually upon objects that are as confined and uninteresting as anything can be. Think of nothing except the word *om* or *mu*, day and night, or, as in Eastern orthodoxy, the name of Jesus. Somehow, in a fashion that is never clearly explained, intense concentration over a period of time brings about a fundamental alteration in the very structure of consciousness. Some say that it brings the surface consciousness to a state of such calm that we can, as it were, see down to the deepest levels of the mind, to a mode of consciousness more basic and natural than that to which we are accustomed. Others say that it is a form of self-hypnotism, giving us the power to control our own mind in such a way that we can think or feel anything we want. Others again say that concentration brings about a state of identity between subject and object, knower and known, in which the sense of the separate ego, the isolated self-conscious subject, disappears.

When I first began to study these things, I was a student in England, and naturally most of my time was given over to reading. I was puzzled as to how concentration such as I've just described could be carried on in the midst of intellectual study. I laid my difficulty before a Japanese Zen master and was amazed to receive the following reply: "It is difficult to conceive the exact idea of exercising Buddhist concentration or meditation in the West. No one can possibly concentrate intentionally upon a given object. That is a fact of truth; try it. Occasionally, one should concentrate on something without one's own intention. That concentration is deep and strong and lasts a long time. Sometimes it reaches to *samadhi*. If we speak philosophically, we might say that we are concentrating constantly, every day. We concentrate on every smallest thought that comes into and passes through our brain. Though it comes and passes so quickly, we never fail to concentrate ourselves in each of those thoughts. In fact, we focus our attention, concentrate, on the strongest thought, that which arouses most interest, that which presents itself at any moment. If it were not the strongest thought, we—of our own attention, using our everyday conscious mind—could not possibly concentrate upon it. Our concentration is always absorbed into the strongest thought. Speaking logically, we say, 'It is of no use to try to concentrate on a given thing,' yet we should concentrate every moment while we are living. In the first stage of meditation, we understand that our egoistic intention to concentrate on something is impossible. Therefore, we train ourselves to concentrate according to the power that is beyond our everyday consciousness, and yet is within us. In this manner we yield entirely to our true or real nature, which connects with all nature. To practice this, we must give up our own intention; shut off, as it were, our own brain action; cease to drive our mind in a egoistic sense. Just let go, as you go with a stream, not rowing your boat with your own strength or purpose. Go with the stream of nature. Do not try to go against the stream. This is practice for a beginner, but using it, you will find entrance into the way."

For me, this answer was an eye-opener. Three things stood out in it. The first, which I had already realized, was that to the degree the act of concentration upon anything is intentional, it is self-frustrating. It is concentrating on concentrating. The second eye-opener was the notion, odd to me, that we are really concentrating all the time upon every successive thought, however brief. In other words, concentration, the absorption of the subject and the object, or vice versa, is the natural state of our consciousness. The third thing that stood out for me is not quite so easy to express, because it seems paradoxical. It is the idea of training ourselves to concentrate without intention, according to the power of nature that is beyond our everyday consciousness, and yet is within us. This apparent paradox becomes intelligible, however, if we have correctly understood the first two points. Trying intentionally to concentrate is self-frustrating because that is what the Zen people call "putting legs on a snake." It is a confusing irrelevance, trying to do what we are already doing. For as the second point reveals, the mind is necessarily and always concentrated already. The problem, therefore, is not so much to concentrate as to prolong concentration upon any one thought or impression. But this must be done naturally, according to the mind's innate mode of functioning, and not by force.

If, in other words, I understand that force or intentional concentration is impossible, if I really know this to be so, and thus give it up, I immediately and automatically acquire the feel of the mind's innate and natural concentration, and so am enabled to use that concentration.

Now, what is the connection between this, the egoistic predicament, and the alteration of normal human consciousness from the egocentric to the universal? I think this connection becomes clear if one looks at the idea of intentional concentration in a wider context, as something more than an occasional attempt to perform a mental exercise. In this wider context, intentional concentration is the mind's almost habitual attempt to concentrate upon or identify itself with whatever is pleasurable. It is the mind's attempt to concentrate or force one's thoughts and feelings into constantly gratifying channels. Furthermore, it is also an attempt to force as much pleasure out of each moment as possible, to attend to it with all one's might, and in general, to dominate the mind with the mind. This is a misuse of the mind. It is an attempt to work the mind in a way that is against its natural functioning. It is like forcing a saw through wood instead of letting it do its own cutting. The good carpenter, letting the saw cut by itself, neither stops cutting nor lets his saw wander from the line. He continues his work as before. But it feels different from when he'd been forcing the saw, for now he is working with the nature of his instruments and media, not against it. This then is what the Zen master meant by shutting off one's own brain action and ceasing to drive one's mind in an egoistic sense. But this is a shutting off that is not the outcome of rigorous effort. On the contrary, it happens automatically once it becomes clear that forcing and driving the mind gets us nowhere, faster and faster.

Now, the constant strain and frustration of forcing the mind is for most human beings an enduring and basic sensation, present in almost everything we do. It is precisely this sensation that constitutes the individual ego, the separate self we believe ourselves to be. Therefore, spiritual disciplines involving prolonged effort of concentration turn out to be very cumbersome, roundabout ways of self-transcendence, however effective they may be in the long run. For ultimately what is needed is not so much the muscle power of the will as a clear intelligence, a clear and undoubted vision of the total absurdity and unnaturalness of using the mind in a forced way, of trying to control the controller by psychological violence.

Compared with ordinary yoga exercises and similar disciplines, seeing the absurdity of using the mind in this unnatural way is relatively easy. Furthermore, in relieving the constant strain that we call the ego, a new sensation of ease and, indeed, naturalness fills the whole of everyday experience. It is an unblocked sensation—which may be experienced or described as the feeling of voidness or oneness with the universe.

If you have a New England conscience, however, you will be quite certain that anything which is easy or which feels easy is wrong. You will glory in effort for its own sake and babble about the inherent splendor of the struggle of the human spirit against nature, thinking it all the more glorious just because it is all so fundamentally tragic. The point being not so much to succeed as to do battle. Not to conquer but to toughen the character.

Perhaps this is to some extent a matter of taste, but for me, all this kind of talk is pompous and asinine. And this may be just because I am an inherently lazy fellow.

Now, there do seem to me to be times when verve and vigor are appropriate. Times when force works with, not against, nature. As Shakespeare said, "There is a tide in the affairs of men, which, taken at the flood, leads on to fortune." But when the tide is not at its flood, when mere brawn is up against granite, the effort to go against nature seems to me not so much tragically splendid as stupid. At best, one could say with the French general of the Charge of the Light Brigade, *"C'est magnifique, mais ce n'est pas la guerre."* To call it splendid is to base one's evaluation of man on his animal strength over what is more characteristically human—his intelligence. This misevaluation is perhaps based on the common distrust of intelligence, on the part of those who lack it, as something tricky, cunning, and weak-spined. But this misevaluation also reduces the standards of human character until they are more applicable to pachyderms and rocks than to human beings. For after all, is the final test of character really just in seeing how much suffering you can take? How much suffering you can endure always depends on how insensitive you are. But to be human is above all to be sensitive. And this means, I think, that the measure of character becomes, among other things, the quality rather than the quantity of your suffering. For the depth and quality of human consciousness is outlined and defined by its borders, beyond which there are things that it cannot take. Thus, our very weaknesses are our strength. As Lao-tzu said, "Suppleness and tenderness are the concomitants of life. Rigidity and hardness are the concomitants of death."

CHAPTER FOUR

Zen and the Art of the Controlled Accident

德 Zen and Taoism in common involve not a system of doctrine—not a set of beliefs as we ordinarily understand religion—but a transformation of consciousness, that is to say, a transformation of the way in which we experience our own existence at every moment. We might say that average individuals, not only in the West but also in the East, have a feeling of themselves as separate from their surroundings—from other people, from the earth, from space. They feel this in ways that are expressed in all the phrases of common speech. We talk about coming *into* the world: "I came into this world." As a matter of fact, we didn't. We came *out of* it, in the same way that an apple comes out of an apple tree—as an expression of the tree. We say, "I am facing facts," as if facts—the things happening around us—were something we confronted as a being alien to and different from us, as if we were meeting them as total strangers.

In the West we talk about the conquest of nature, which is a very hostile phrase. To understand the Chinese point of view, let's consider the relationship between bees and flowers. There are no flowers where there are no bees. There are no bees where there are no flowers. They go together, like our head and our feet. Or as the head of a cat goes with the tail of a cat. If we watched a cat walk past a narrow crack in a fence, we would first see the head, and then the tail. And if the cat turned around and walked past again, we would see first the head, and then the tail. If we had never seen a cat before, we might assume that our experience of the head of the cat was one event and that our experience of the tail was another event. We might assume that they were separate from each other, and only related as cause to effect. But if our crack in the fence were widened, we would see that it was all one cat and that the head and the tail go together.

We have a way of attending to life, which we call "conscious attention," and it's like a narrow crack in a fence. We can think of only one thing at a time. Our speech reflects this. This is one of our ways of experiencing the world: bit by bit. A chicken, for example, does not come out of an egg as a cut-up fryer; it comes out as an entire chicken, and if we want to eat it, we have to cut it up. But the world that we live in and experience is not cut up into separate things and events. It all goes together in the same way that the bees and the flowers go together, but we don't notice it. We have a way of thinking that splits everything up;

we feel separate from the whole domain of nature. The disciplines of Taoism and Zen are supposed to change our consciousness in such a way that we no longer feel that we're an isolated unit locked up within a bag of skin. Instead, we actually experience the fact that our real self—the real us—is everything that there is; that all reality is concentrated and expressing itself at the point known as our personal organism.

There are, of course, intimations of this in the West, just as there are in the East. For example, there is Western astrology—something that is partly superstitious in my view. Astrology does not seem to me to be an effective method of predicting the future. But it has some sense to it, in that when a child is born, the parents consult an astrologer, and the astrologer draws a map of the baby's soul, or character. The map consists of a symbolic picture of the universe as it was the moment the child was born. And if the picture of the child's soul is the same thing as a picture of the universe, the soul is not inside the body. The body, rather, is within the soul. Your soul is the entire pattern of reality—of everything that is—focused at the point you experience as "here and now," just as you can focus the sun on a small point with a magnifying glass.

In the science of ecology, which studies the relationship between organisms and environments, one is acutely aware—in an intellectual way—that an organism, whether human or animal or insect or plant, is not merely something "in" an environment, as we are "in" this room, but rather that the organism and its environment behave *together*. They go with each other. The sense of the saying in the Gospel's "Figs do not grow on thistles, nor grapes on thorns" has this application. So does the idea that human beings must grow in a cosmos that is itself intelligent. If human beings are intelligent—and we define "intelligence" as the human way of thinking and feeling—then the universe must be intelligent, too. We do not get an intelligent organism in an unintelligent environment. An apple tree does not grow apples all the time; planets and stars do not produce life all the time. But every so often they do. So if an apple tree may be said to "apple," this kind of universe in which we live can be said to "people." It is a peopling world, and we go with it. The problem is that we don't ordinarily feel that way. We feel that we're strangers on the earth, and so we talk about the conquest of nature and facing facts and all that nonsense.

So what is proposed here is the transformation of everyday consciousness into a new kind of sensation—the sensation that what is going on *outside* you is all one process with what is going on *inside* you and that you are all there is.

We shall not necessarily know this objectively, the way we know an object is across the room. Let me give an illustration. Conscious attention, which is the faculty we use most to get around, is rather like the headlight of a car. The headlight illumines the road in front but does not shine on the wiring that connects it with the battery, and the battery with the engine. In just that way we are not ordinarily aware of how we are aware. As a result, we don't understand our connection to the world—we are unaware of what our real self is. Therefore, we get anxious. We fear that death may be the end of us, and that somehow we shall just pass out of this world altogether, and that will be that.

This is, of course, the purest superstition, because everyone, in fact, is indestructible. We as individual organisms—as what we call physical bodies—come and go like leaves on a tree, but the tree remains: and we are the tree. In the saying of Jesus, "I am the vine, you are the branches." That *I am*—"Before Abraham was, I am"—is the self, and what the Hindus call the *brahman* and the Chinese call the *tao*. And the tao is curious. The basic idea is that life is a flowing dance that consists of going on and stopping—what the Chinese call *yang* and *yin*. Yang is the southern, or sunny, side of a mountain. It is the sunny, south side of a mountain or the north bank of a river, wherever the sun falls. Yin is then the shadow side. Now imagine a mountain with only one side or a river with only one bank. Nobody can.

Life is entirely a game of "now you see it, now you don't," on, off—like the crests and troughs of waves. You cannot have a wave unless you have both a crest and a trough. This is true in hydraulics and in electronics. Without the one, you do not have the other. And so the relationship between these two things is called "mutual arriving," which is the most important term in Taoist philosophy. It is symbolized by the yin/yang symbol, which means "reciprocal" or "mutual," and it's based on an old ideogram for a plant growing, arising, coming into being. The fundamental idea is that the yang and the yin come into being together. You never find one without the other. There is a kind of secret conspiracy, like Tweedledum and Tweedledee agreeing to have a battle. So although yin and yang are different—in the way that front and back are different, high and low are different, being and nonbeing are different—they always go together.

So "to be, or not to be" is not the universal question. It is the question for the West. For all existentialist thinking, "to be, or not to be" really *is* the question. And when it is the question, man must necessarily be anxious. The moment we know that we exist, we face the possibility that we might cease to be. And so we tremble. But when "to be, or not to be" is not the question, we as individuals come to feel that we are not something strange in this world. We come to feel that we are an *expression* of the world, and that the world is us. We are more than our physical bodies. Our physical body is "us," in one sense, and has a certain degree of independence. But at the same time, it is an expression of the entire universe, as a wave is an expression of the ocean. The ocean waves to us and says, "Yoo-hoo, I am here." In the same way, the whole cosmos waves at us and says, "Hi," and waves at the other waves and says, "Hello, glad to meet you." But we are all really the one center expressing itself, playing in an infinite variety of ways.

"Well, what does this lead to," you ask, "in terms of practical consequences?" For one thing, it leads to a respect for the external world as one's own body. It leads to knowing how to get in tempo with the world, to act with rather than against the grain. And this is the most important lesson that ancient China has to teach the modern technological West. Because in technology, we have a fantastic power for altering—not only the external environment but ourselves. Through technology, neurosurgery, and drugs, we can affect our brains and begin to interfere with our own characters.

The most asinine thing for us to do would be to live in this lovely environment and spoil it by living in it. So if you were a skillful architect who worked on the principle of the tradition of Taoist and Zen architecture, you would go to the environment in which you planned to build—let us say it is a great hill—and say to it, "Good morning." You might even bow and say, "I want to live here, what kind of house would you like to have on you?" And the hill might answer, "I'd like a house that would disrupt me as little as possible, because I have a game going on here. I have a huge complexity of plants and insects and small animals who manage to keep me here. These plants prevent avalanches, and so on." And the hill would suggest to the sensitive artist, or architect, a way to build a house that wouldn't interfere with the ecology of the hill. And the architect would think, "How will I do this?" and come up with a solution.

But instead of being sensitive to the game being played by the hill, we go into the hills with bulldozers and terrace them to make room for houses that are appropriate only for flatland. We need the flatland for agriculture, so people should live in the hills. But in order to do so, we have to understand how to treat hills. Look at the way the hills on the north and the east sides of Kyoto have been civilized. They have the most beautiful way of concealing houses in the hills, so you hardly know they're there. They didn't use bulldozers. Or the exquisite way Japanese farmers have adapted their land to the landscape with contour farming, so that a mountainous country, of which 80 percent of the land is nonarable, has been made 80 percent self-supporting. They farm the sea; the Japanese eat seaweed and other things that very few of us in the West will eat. And all along the California coast there is a fantastic abundance of kelp, which is delicious if you know how to cook it. But we have to learn these lessons, because we're going to have a terrible time if we don't. This is the principle that is called in Taoist philosophy *wu wei,* which means "not to force things." I've come to believe this is the best English translation. It is sometimes translated as "not doing, no artificiality, no interference." But our word *forcing,* as in a forced laugh, forcing a lock, forced

behavior, forced kindness, forced love—forcing in that sense—
is the opposite of wu wei. *Wu wei* means action in accordance
with the character of the moment.

You can't avoid interfering with the world. Everything you
do alters your environment. And nobody knows this more than
a chemist or physicist. The scientist realizes that whenever he so
much as inspects the behavior of electrons, the very means of
his inspection will alter the way in which they behave. Shine a
light on something to look at it, and that bombardment of light
affects your subject, especially at the nuclear level. This process
goes on constantly. To know things is to change them. You
cannot escape interfering. Therefore, the idea is to learn how to
interfere skillfully. That is the meaning of wu wei: how to act
with the grain of the world.

There is one other idea that has to be understood, and that
is *li*. It is a Chinese term that goes along with wu wei. It is not
found in ancient Taoism—though it is based in a Taoist view of
the world—but appears later, in Ch'an, or Chinese Zen.

Li is a fascinating expression. It originally meant "markings
in jade, grain in wood, fiber in muscle." Western scholars have
translated it as "reason, or principle," but this is not a very good
translation. *Li* is the word used in China to designate the character of the order of nature. So, our scholars tend to translate it
as "the laws of nature." But the Chinese have no words that we
can correctly translate as "the laws of nature," because they do

not look upon nature as obeying laws. They look upon it as orderly, but not legal.

We cannot write down the rules for something like fair play. We know them without being told, and they are too subtle to be put into words. In the same way, we cannot precisely describe the human nervous system. It is too complicated and will always elude us, although we get closer and closer to describing it.

The judge who understands that justice goes beyond the law is informed by the principle of li. Li means the markings in jade. When you get a piece of jade and look at its markings, you do not think of them as chaotic. When you see a dirty old ash-tray with cigarette butts in it, and rolled up bits of paper, you know it's a mess. But when you study the patterns on rocks or the shapes of clouds or the outlines of trees, you know that they're not orderly in the sense of being symmetrical, but you know that they're beautiful. Painters, in the Western tradition, copy clouds and say, "Well, there's a picture. I know what clouds are about." But clouds don't *mean* anything. Clouds are not a picture of anything. They are just clouds. They are just clouding.

There is a poem with the line "Blue mountains are spontaneously blue mountains, white clouds are spontaneously white clouds." They just do that; it is their game. We know that they are not chaotic—we recognize that they possess an order—but we cannot quite pin down wherein that order lies. We know it is order, and we can analyze it physically and chemically—we can learn about surface tension and bubble formation and why clouds form the way they do—but we get only an approximate understanding of the order that underlies these phenomena. When surveyors measure land, they reduce it to so many small triangles. They measure those triangles, and that measures the land. But that is only an approximation; we never get it exactly right. So, there is always an ungraspable and indefinable principle of order in things, and that is li. And that explains why Chinese art appreciates, in all that it does, a certain element of the uncontrolled.

Some Chinese painters like to let everything go wild. But the ideal they are all aiming at—and you have to be a tremendous master to achieve it—is to let everything go wild within limits, to create a situation that is orderly overall but that allows for unexpected, random surprises. And they look upon daily life in exactly the same way.

Bees are quite remarkable for this reason: every bee does exactly what it feels like doing, and yet the hive is orderly. Imagine that. Suppose you could get up every day and live in such a way that you always did exactly what you wanted. You didn't pay attention to schedules or to what anybody else was doing. You simply did as you pleased. And it so happened that what you felt like doing was what everybody else felt like doing, and this produced an orderly performance. The bees, in a sense, are in that situation. To follow the Tao is to learn the art of doing

exactly what you feel like doing. At the same time it is wu wei—
it does not force; it does not impose.

To do that—to act naturally—we have to understand
another Chinese word, *tzuran,* which means "that which is so of
itself." We translate *tzuran* as "nature," although it is very unlike
our word *nature.* It means "that which happens naturally." When
we say that something "comes naturally" or that something is
"second nature" to us, we approach the meaning of *tzuran.* In
his writings on the tao, Lao-tzu says, "The Tao's method is to be
so of itself."

We have in the West an image of the universe as something
that is being run by somebody. The Lord God is in control. He
made it all; He engineered it all; He understands it; He remains
in control. The Chinese view of the universe is exactly the opposite. It looks upon the universe as not being controlled at all, as
being perfectly orderly of itself. So, Lao-tzu says, "The great Tao
flows everywhere, both to the left and to the right. It loves and
nourishes all things, but does not lord it over them. And when
good things are accomplished, it lays no claim to them."

I know, for example, of a religious order in Japan in which
there are about two hundred men and women who live very
simply, in families, and they are fantastically happy people. They
run their gardens and farms, and buzz around town visiting
people who are sick or otherwise incapable of caring for themselves. They come right in and clean the whole house; they do

all the washing and clean out the toilets, and then they just dis-appear. It is a very curious thing, but they just vanish.

There is a poem in Zen which says, "Entering the forest, he does not disturb a blade of grass. / Entering the water, he does not make a ripple." He was so in accord with the scene, and he flowed so easily through it, that nobody noticed.

Water not disturbed by waves settles down of itself. A mirror not covered with dust is clear and bright. The mind should be like this.

Many people think that living the spontaneous, or com-pletely natural, life, as it is understood by these Far Eastern philosophers, means to act according to whim. Around A.D. 1000, for example, there was a great Zen monk who had a pecu-liar way of painting. He had long hair, and he would get very drunk on rice wine. Then he would soak his hair in ink and slosh it all over the paper. He would do a Rorschach test on the result, decide what kind of landscape it was, and put on the fin-ishing touches. And suddenly, out of this apparent mess, a great landscape would be evoked. And the whole art lay in applying the finishing touches.

If a person who is untrained in painting makes a mess with the brush, it is liable to be nothing more than a mess. Whereas if a person who has had the feeling of painting in him for a long time makes a mess with a brush, it will look interesting. That is why if you try to copy the best painters in modern abstract, nonobjective painting, you will find it very difficult to do so. For there is more to spontaneity than caprice and disorder.

Wouldn't it be great if we could live absolutely on the spur of the moment? To never make any particular plans unless we made them spontaneously; to never worry about whether we had made the right decision; to never wonder if we'd been selfish or unselfish; to never hesitate. One of the great applications of Zen was to the art of fencing. In fencing, we learn to be spontaneous, because here, of all places, it is true that he who hesitates is lost. If we are engaged in combat and stop to think about what sort of a defense or attack we ought to make, we're finished.

The way they teach spontaneity in fencing is very interesting. As a student, of course, you live with your teacher. And in the beginning you are given a janitorial job—you clean up, wash dishes, put away bedding. And while you're going about your daily business, the master surprises you with a practice sword made of four strips of bamboo tied loosely together. He hits you suddenly, out of nowhere. And you're expected to defend yourself with anything available—with the bedding, with the broom, with the pots and pans. But you never know when the attack is coming or from what direction. And you begin to get tense. You go everywhere on alert, watching, waiting to see which direction the blow will come from. You go down a certain passage, feeling certain that the master is lurking around the far corner. You're all set for him, and then you're suddenly hit from behind. So eventually you just give up. There is absolutely no way to prepare yourself for these attacks, and you finally start wandering around with the feeling that if you're going to be hit, you're going to be hit. And then you're ready to begin fencing. Because if you prepare for an attack from a specific direction, and the attack comes from elsewhere, you have to withdraw from the direction in which you had expected it before you can respond to the attack. And by then it's too late.

So, instead, you must develop a mind of no expectation. That state is called *mushin,* or *munin.* This is a very important Zen expression. *Mushin* almost means "an empty mind." You could also call it "no heart," because the character *shin* means both "heart" and "mind." But it isn't quite the same as our word *heartless.* Nor is it the same as our word *mindless,* in the sense of "stupid." To be in the state of mushin is to have a mind like a mirror. Of this, a Taoist sage said, "The perfect man employs his mind as a mirror. It grasps nothing, it refuses nothing. It receives but does not keep." When something passes in front of a mirror, the mirror reflects it instantly. The mirror doesn't wait to reflect it. The Taoists also say, "When the moon rises, all bodies of water instantly reflect the moon." They don't bother with irrelevant physics about the speed of light. They say, "When you clap your hands, the sound issues immediately. It doesn't stop to consider whether it will issue." And similarly, when a flint is struck, sparks issue instantly. To emulate this, you cannot try to be quick. If a Zen master corners you with a peculiar situation—if he puts you in a quandary, expecting a spontaneous action—do not try to hurry. I have watched Suzuki wait a whole minute before answering a question. But he did not hesitate. He was not at all embarrassed by this wait. He can answer with silence just as well as with a formal response. The point is, Do something.

Two young Americans who wanted to study Zen were taken to interview the master by a Japanese monk who acted as interpreter, and one of the Americans had some experience. After they had tea together, the master said, in a very easy way, "Well, what do you gentlemen know about Zen?" And the American threw his fan, which he hadn't unfolded, straight at the master's face. The master moved slightly to one side, and the fan went right through the rice-paper wall behind him. The master laughed like a child. That is the sort of game they get into.

Once a master was going through a forest with a group of students, picked up a tree branch, and turned to one of his students. "What is it?" he asked, and the student hesitated. So the master hit him with the branch. Then the master turned quickly to another student and repeated, "What is it?" And the student said, "Give it to me. Let me see it and I'll tell you." So the master tossed the branch to the student, and the student took it and hit the master.

Now, you may think all this is kind of rough stuff, so let me give you another story on a rather different level.

A certain Zen priest was at a big party. And dinner was being served by a geisha girl who was so elegant and so skillful in serving that he suspected she might have had some Zen training. So he decided to try her out. He nodded to her, and she immediately came to his place, sat down in front of his little low table, and bowed. He said, "I would like to give you a present." And she said, "I would be most honored." There were hibachis on the tables—with iron chopsticks for the coals—and he took out a piece of charcoal with the chopsticks and offered it to her. She wound the long sleeves of her kimono around her hands and took the charcoal. Then she went to the kitchen, disposed of the charcoal, changed her burnt robe, and came back. She sat down in front of the master, bowed again, and said, "I would like to give you a present." The master said, "I would be most honored." So she picked up the iron chopsticks and offered him a piece of charcoal. And he pulled out a cigarette and said, "That is just what I wanted." And he lit the cigarette.

The master's spontaneity in that situation was like that of a good comedian who, in a completely unprepared way, can turn any situation into a jest. There are many experts—like Dorothy Parker—in that sort of repartee, and in Zen it has been developed to a very high degree. But it requires a protected, highly disciplined environment. If you suddenly started to act on the spur of the moment, without the slightest deliberation, people would avoid you and call the police. In the practice of Zen, therefore, you begin to act spontaneously within the confines of a monastery or school, in a community that understands the game. In a Zen environment there are rigid rules, but there are also certain instances when all those rules go hang. The point is this: when you first begin to act spontaneously, you're not used to it, and your responses are usually unintelligent and inappropriate. When, through practice, it becomes second nature to act in the state of mushin—or no-mind—without deliberation, you will find that you are accustomed to responding quite appropriately, as the Zen master did in lighting his cigarette from the charcoal.

So, in the art of swordsmanship when the student gives up defending himself and preparing his mind for attack, he achieves a mirror mind. This is also likened to a wooden barrel full of water. When you make a hole in the barrel, the water instantly flows out the hole. The water is always available to flow—it doesn't have to choose. You could also say that mushin is what Krishnamurti calls "choicelessness." *Choice,* in this sense, is not quite the same thing as *decision. Choice* means dithering. You know those people who wiggle their pens a little—their pens dither over the paper—before they start to write. In the same way, many people constantly dither in their lives because they are anxious, and dithering is an expression of anxiety. "To be, or not to be: that is the question." But what is the question about, "to be, or not to be"? "To be" and "not to be" go together. They arise mutually.

So the structure of a Zen community allows you to learn how to act without deliberation—to return, in a sense, to the state of innocence. This does not mean that you give up thinking. It doesn't mean that you become an anti-intellectual. One can learn—in the later phases of Zen training—how to intellectualize spontaneously, how to think and deliberate spontaneously. The saying is "Stand or walk as you will, but whatever you do, don't wobble." This is difficult because the human mind is a feedback system, and feedback has a peculiar susceptibility to nervousness. There was a young man who said, "Though it seems that I know that I know, what I would like to see is the 'I' that knows 'me' when I know that I know that I know." In this way, we think about thinking and we worry about worrying; and when that really gets bad, we worry because we worry about worrying. Now this is exactly analogous to the kinds of vibrations that are set up in certain mechanical systems. On television I once told the audience, "I'm going to show you a picture of anxiety," and I asked the cameraman to turn the camera on the studio monitor. And when he aimed the camera at the monitor's screen—when he began to take a picture of the picture, as it were—the screen began to oscillate, and jagged lines began to dance across it. Now, that is what is meant by hesitation, attachment, blocking—all the things Zen discipline is designed to overcome. It is because the human being has such a peculiarly and beautifully organized nervous system, with a tremendously subtle brain capable of all kinds of thinking about thinking. You can drive yourself crazy this way, and this is what we are doing. Our civilization and our social institutions reflect this in hundreds of ways. This is true of any civilization because all civilization is based on the development of self-consciousness and feedback—that is to say, on the properties of self-control, of learning to criticize and correct what you have done. But who is the critic? Is the critic reliable? If you criticize yourself, who will criticize the critic? To put it another way, who will guard the guards? Who will take care of the policemen? Who will govern the president? That is the big problem. The Chinese and the Japanese got tied up in it because they were both very high orders of civilization. And when this happens, there has to be a break. Somebody has to start throwing things.

So Zen functions in the Japanese culture as a means of liberation from the tangle of being too civilized. The Japanese tend to be tremendously concerned with propriety, good manners, and keeping up with the Joneses. Frequently in Japan when friends meet or take leave, they say "Ah, so," and one bows, and the other bows, and the first bows again, and it goes back and forth, each trying to see who gets the last bow. They also worry terribly about gifts. When visiting, it is customary to arrive with a gift, and the guest will wonder, "Is our gift as nice as the last one they gave us? Is it suitable for the occasion? Is there some symbolism in this gift that connects with the recipient's name or birthday?" They think about such things interminably. And, thus, the ordinary culture has a great deal of social nervousness in it. People giggle. You often see girls covering their mouths as if to say, "I'm not really giggling." All sorts of funny things happen because of this immense social awareness and nervousness. And Zen breaks that up. Only it does so in a way that has high artistry to it.

In the history of ceramics, the Chinese developed some of the most elegant work imaginable. You are probably aware of the great work of the Sung and Korean potters. They often used gorgeous, textured greens, and many of their pieces look almost as if they have been carved out of jade. That led to the high techniques of the Ming dynasty, with translucent porcelain, white clay, and the most subtle designs of all. And that style went on to Japan, filling the houses of the very rich people you find in books like *The Tale of Genji*. The lovely things they had around their houses were unbelievable—the lacquer, the boxes in pure gold. It was delicious stuff. But it got to the point where it was like having too many éclairs and ice cream. And the people who practiced Zen suddenly developed an eye for the beauty of the ordinary.

There were two reasons for this. One was that they became fascinated with what happens spontaneously—with what pattern a brush would make when handled roughly, for instance, and the hairlines were allowed to show. And second, because they practiced *zazen,* which is sitting quietly with a completely open mind. Zazen gradually sharpens your senses, until you start seeing and hearing things with astonishing clarity. There is a famous haiku poem: "The old pond, / a frog jumps in, / plop." In Japanese, that *plop* is a phrase that means the sound of the water. There is another haiku just like it: "In the dark forest, / a berry drops, / the sound of the water." Someone suddenly realized that the sound of water is marvelous all by itself.

Or consider the cheapest Korean rice bowls—the poorest, cheapest kind, for peasants to eat out of. It suddenly struck one of these Zen masters that these bowls were incomparably beautiful objects. Nobody had been aware of this before. They also had the simplest bamboo ladles, and one day somebody noticed that this ordinary, everyday kitchen utensil was just lovely. And in the same way they found that it was quite as satisfactory to listen to the kettle boiling as to listen to an elaborate concert.

So a man named Sanuriku and others began to have parties for a very few guests in primitive, mud huts and in their gardens. Using the simplest utensils—each carefully chosen by a superb artist—they would sit and drink tea and enjoy the uncomplicated life. And so was born the tea ceremony.

The advent of the tea ceremony was terribly important for the Japanese. It was going back to the primitive, after they'd grown sick of too much civilization. And yet, really, it was going *on* to the primitive, rather than back, because it happened in the context of an extremely refined civilization and culture. They were not barbarians. Today, the tea ceremony is an extremely congenial get-together, full of easy conversation, simple and unostentatious manners, and lovely things to look at.

I was once present at a tea ceremony in Japan celebrated by an American Zen monk. He was a mountaineer and always had with him the kind of equipment you take into the mountains. And I said to him, "It would be very nice to have a tea ceremony. You did it once before, and it was so pleasant, would you serve it again?" And he said, "Yes, by all means." The first time he had served the tea ceremony in the simple and direct style of Zen monks. This is much more comfortable than the way the tea ceremony is served by all those well-educated ladies who titter about on tiptoe, hoping they won't make a mistake. This time the American monk came in with a mountaineering primer stove and an old paint pot with an aluminum mug inside it. He set these down and ritually pumped up the stove. Then he took the aluminum mug out of the paint pot, poured water into the pot, and set it on the stove. He did everything in the style of tea ceremony, even though he was using a dirty old primer stove. Suddenly, the stove began to flame like the god Futo, and he mixed the tea with a whisk in the traditional way and then handed us the aluminum cup. He had all the perfect, lovely manners. It is the custom, after you have drunk, to pass around the utensils for inspection. We found that the aluminum cup had the year 1945 stamped on it, and we got into a long discussion about styles of aluminum cups made in 1945. It was the funniest thing, and it was also a complete makeover of the tea ceremony into the modern idiom.

The tea drunk in a tea ceremony is a powdered green tea that you don't steep like ordinary tea. You whisk it and a small amount of hot water into a froth. They call it liquid jade, and it's a bit of an acquired taste for most Westerners. It tastes a little like a mixture of matai tea and Guinness stout. But when you get used to it, it's very invigorating, and a strong mixture of it is a good thing to use if you want to stay awake all night and work.

Legend has it that Zen monks developed an interest in tea because they needed to stay awake during their practice of meditation. Bodhidharma is always drawn with his eyes wide-open, and there is a reason for this: he fell asleep while meditating, and he was so furious when he woke up that he cut his eyelids off. They dropped to the ground, and up came the first tea plants. That is why their leaves are shaped like eyelids and why tea has been drunk for staying awake ever since. So tea is the Buddhist drink, just like wine is the Christian drink, coffee is the Islamic drink, and milk, the Hindu drink. Every religion has its drink.

CHAPTER FIVE

The Democratization of Buddhism

徳 So then, out of this kind of appreciation, born of stillness and a delight in seeing how nature takes its course, came the entire cult of Zen art, with its special kind of primitivity, its special ceramics, its special calligraphic styles, and its special gardens—all of which are manifestations of "the controlled accident."

Consider this water jar. The bottom has been left unglazed. But look, see how the glaze has been allowed to run. It's not at all what we would call neat. I have watched a man pick up an unpainted plate and, as he applies the glaze, just go *whoosh* once with the brush—and it's done. There is another man who glazes by wood smoke, and he may put as many as eleven hundred pieces in his kiln. He wraps each piece in straw, and wherever the straw touches, it leaves a splash of orange against a purple background. The straw arranges itself according to the nature of straw. It doesn't follow strict human direction. And when he opens up the kiln and brings the things out, he looks eagerly to see what the straw has done.

This principle of letting glaze run to see what happens is wu wei. It is noninterference. This is mushin also: no-purpose. It can also be translated as "no specific intent." And, of course, sometimes this noninterference doesn't work. The master picks up the plate or bowl and says, "This is not very interesting," and rejects it.

What then are the canons of taste that decide whether he accepts one of these accidents or rejects it? Because here an additional principle of control enters. In the practice of calligraphy, for instance, a man may sit down with a huge pile of paper in front of him and do piece after piece after piece, and if it isn't just right, he throws it away. Eventually he finds one that is just right.

There is a famous story of a Zen master who was doing calligraphy and had a very smart monk who was his assistant standing beside him. And the monk said, "Uh-uh," to each one the master did. "You could do better than that." And "Oh, no, no, come now, you know you can do much better than that." His master got more and more furious, and when the monk had to go out to the *benjo*—to the toilet—he thought, "Quick, while he is away. . . ." And he did another piece. When the monk came back and looked at it, he said, "A masterpiece."

So what determines this element of selection? How do you

know which drawing or bowl or plate to choose? Take another example. There was a tea caddy, made out of clay, and when Sanu Riku was having tea ceremony, he saw this tea caddy and made no comment on it. And the owner was so disappointed that he smashed it. But one of his friends picked the broken pieces out of the trash can and took them to a mender, saying, "Look, mend this with gold." And the mender used gold cement and put the caddy back together, and it had spidery lines of gold all over its surface. And when Riku saw it, he was just enchanted, and it became one of the most valuable tea caddies in Japanese collections—spidery lines of gold just following the apparently chance marks produced when it was smashed.

There was a competition at the Art Institute of Chicago, in a sculpture class: each student was given a cubic foot of plaster of paris and told to do something with it. The prize was won by a woman who looked at this cube and said, "It has no character, it doesn't want to be anything." So she flung it on the floor, smashing it all up. She made dents in it and banged off the corners and put cracks in it. Then she looked at it again and said, "Ah, now I know what it wants to be." And so she followed the grain in it, as it were, made by all these cracks, and she produced a marvelous piece of sculpture.

There is a very ingenious sculptor by the name of Donald Hord, who is a master at following the grain in wood. It seems to suggest to him the muscles and the flow of the kind of body that he is making.

Well, that's the thing. When a master decides whether an accident has come off, what he looks for is this: the piece to be the perfect harmony of man and nature, of order and randomness.

There is a curious thing about the human mind. When we play games, we get the most fascination from those that satisfactorily combine skill and chance. Games like bridge and poker have an admirable combination of these two elements. And we can go on playing those games again and again, because we don't feel completely at the mercy of chance, as we do with dice—unless we cheat—and we don't feel completely at the mercy of skill, as we do with chess. So there is a sort of optimum middle where order and randomness go together. That is what a master is looking for in a work of art: the optimal combination of order and randomness.

Art works such as Persian miniatures, the jewelry of Cellini, or Chinese porcelain emphasize skill too much; they contain too much order. They are like those houses you go into where you dare not put an ash in the tray because everything is so clean and so tidy that you can't touch it. One prefers a house that looks a little lived in. It is more genial, more comfortable; it somehow invites you to sit down and put your feet on the table. At the other extreme, however, is the kind of home where everything is covered in dirt, filthy clothes are thrown in the corner, and the people have paint all over them. That goes too far in the opposite direction. We don't want that, either. What we want is that curious thing in the middle.

Now, the most difficult thing to do is hold to the middle. It's like walking a tightrope. That is why the path of Buddhism is called the razor's edge. In the course of history, what happens when this kind of work becomes fashionable is that people begin to affect these styles. For example, Seshu, the great master ink-painter, would sometimes paint with a handful of straw instead of a brush, in order to get the sort of rough effect that he wanted. But later on there came people who could take an ordinary paintbrush and so exactly ink that brush that it would give precisely the messy effect that imitated Seshu's discovery. They also learned to ink a brush in such a way—and this is terribly decadent—that they could dab grapes on a vine and have dark ink where the shadow was supposed to be, and no ink at all where the highlights were supposed to be. That is when they started getting mixed up with Western ideas about shadows and perspective. They didn't have that earlier. But they were so skilled in the handling of ink that they would do this sort of thing, imitating all the so-called rough, natural effects of the great Zen artists. Today in Japan a younger generation of artists has decided that it's time to break away from all that.

Or imagine modern haiku parties and the writing of

modern haiku poetry. Bashō who was the great seventeenth-century master of haiku, said, "Get a three-foot-high child to write haiku," because haiku are the sort of direct, guileless things that children say. But now, instead, there are magazines devoted to haiku poetry. In every issue there will be ten thousand haikus written by people all over the country, and they are so stilted and so affected that one wishes one had never *heard* of haiku.

The same thing is starting over here. You should see the entries they get in the haiku competitions that Japan Airlines and others sponsor. After a while, it all becomes dated, stilted. And somewhere, again, a new thing has to break out, which it is always doing.

But there is no formula for fixing the stilted thing so that you can do it again and again and again. The moment you start doing it again and again, it isn't the same thing anymore. The real thing has escaped.

Do you remember when, some time ago, there was a fashion for having wrought-iron fish—just the outline of the fish. Some artist originally put this fish together, and it looked great. But then you suddenly found them in every gift shop and dime store in the world, and they looked perfectly terrible.

So this is the mysterious thing—not only in the arts but in lifestyles, in everything—as soon as you ask, "What is the technique for getting this thing?" and people tell you, "Well, this is how to do it," the real thing is gone. It's the same in education. And in music. The moment you start teaching something, what question are you asking?

Is there some method whereby in our schools we could produce from each music department, at every graduation ceremony, three musicians of the stature of Bach or Mozart? If we knew how to do that, such knowledge would prevent us from being surprised by the work of these people.

There is a Zen poem that says, "If you ask where the flowers come from, even the God of Spring doesn't know." Certainly the God of Spring should know where the flowers come from. The truth of the matter, though, is He doesn't. And in the same way, if you asked the Lord God, "How do You create the universe?" He would say, "I have no special method."

This is known in Zen as *budji,* the most difficult virtue to attain. *Budji* means "nothing special" or "no business" or "no artificiality." Budji is when something does not stand out like a sore thumb. But it is absolutely different from being modest. A budji person may be immodest, in the sense that if he knows he can do something well he just says he can. Budji is the mysterious quality of "no special method." Because if there is a special method—if we know the method and we know it infallibly—it ceases to be interesting. There are no surprises left. And the moment the element of surprise is gone, the zest for life is gone.

That is why it is very difficult to teach Zen to yourself—

because you cannot easily surprise yourself. The essence of this kind of Zen spontaneity is response to a surprise. You don't know what the master is going to do, and he surprises you. It's like trying to cure hiccups. It's very difficult to cure yourself because when you pat yourself on the back, you know when you're going to do it. You're ready for it. But when somebody else comes up and slams you on the back, it is a surprise. And what you needed was a surprise. Or like a joke: what makes you laugh is the element of surprise. That is why jokes are not funny after they have been explained. So, in the same way, all these Zen stories, if explained, have no effect. They are intended to produce what I would call metaphysical laughter. But this can come only as a surprise. And to be surprised . . . well, there is no way of premeditating it.

You are probably familiar with *Zen in the Art of Archery*, by Eugene Herrigel. He had to learn to pull the bowstring in the manner of the Japanese archer and let it go, but not on purpose. He had to let it go without thinking first, "I'll let it go," and then let go. He had to let it go unintentionally. And that really bugged Herrigel. How do you do something without intention, especially if you're aiming at a target? Well, the point is that if you think before you shoot, it's too late. The target has moved. That is why we have beginner's luck. If you simply point at something without thinking, as if your finger were a gun, you could probably hit whatever you point at.

I will never forget the first time I ever used a slingshot. A friend of mine was with me and was aiming carefully but not hitting the target. And I just picked it up and *ping*, I hit it. But I couldn't do it again. So, the beginner has a certain kind of naturalness.

There was a master by the name of Ikkyu, who was a great leg-puller. And he had in front of his house a very gnarled, contorted pine tree—one of the things that the Japanese really love. And he put up a notice beside it that read "I, Ikkyu, will pay one hundred yen"—which was a fair amount of money in those days—"to anyone who can see this tree straight." Well, soon there was a whole crowd of people around that tree, lying on the ground, twisting their necks and looking at it from all sorts of angles, and there was absolutely no way of seeing the tree with a straight trunk. Ikkyu had a friend named Rosen, who was a priest of another sect. A smart boy went over to see him and asked, "What about Master Ikkyu's tree?"

"Oh," said Rosen, "it is perfectly simple. You go tell him the answer to seeing the tree straight is to look straight at it." So, the boy returned to Ikkyu and said, "I claim the reward. You see the trunk straight by looking straight at it." And Ikkyu looked at him in a funny way and forked over the hundred yen, saying, "I think you have been talking to Rosen down the street."

Now, in that way, just look straight at it. Here is the bowstring—let go of it. Don't get sidetracked into all this fimblefambling, mimble-mambling jumble humble about the right technique of letting go of it. Just let go of it, damn it. But that's very difficult. It is as is if I were to say to you, "Now, everybody, let's be unself-conscious."

So, at last you learn to let go of the thing, and you are again as a child. This is original innocence. This is the meaning of the answer when a Zen master was asked, "What do you do here in this Zen institution?" The master said, "We eat when hungry, and we sleep when tired." "But," the questioner replied, "that is being just like everybody else. They all do that." The master answered, "They do not. When they eat, they do not eat. They think of all sorts of extraneous matters. When they tire, they do not sleep. They dream all kinds of dreams."

Nobody ever transforms himself into an enlightened pattern of life by dividing himself into two pieces—Good I and Bad Me, wherein Good I preaches to Bad Me and tries to make him over. If a human being were divided, we would be like a rider on a horse. The rider is the soul, and the horse is the body; or the rider is reason, and the horse is passion—the rider is control, and the horse is the uncontrolled. In other words, we have the opposition of the ego allied with the superego, trying to ride the ego aligned with the id. Freud's metaphors and his construction of the psychic anatomy are derived from Plato, with the image of the soul riding the animal horse. Now this metaphor is a total failure, because there is a secret connection—a sort of backstairs, as it were—between Good I and Bad Me. Good I can look down at Bad Me and say, "Uh-uh-uh, you oughtn't to be like that." But all the time, Bad Me is sending its energy up the backstairs to Good I, and motivating Good I to go "Uh-uh-uh" at Bad Me. If it were not for the energy of Bad Me, I would be better, one thinks. I'd be more proud of myself.

So there is something about self-conscious spirituality—about religions involving preaching and moralizing and talking to oneself in a split and divided way; Good I against Bad Me—that is profoundly phony.

One of the main streams of the Buddhist way of life is what might be called the religion of nonreligion: to find, to demonstrate, to convey the most highly spiritual through what is the most everyday and ordinary, and to make no division between the two. So you might say the more everyday it is, the more truly spiritual it is, and the more it appears to be spiritual—that is to say, something different from, aside from, apart from everyday life—the more false that kind of spirituality will be.

This reaches a peak in the history of Japanese culture in the seventeenth century, when there were four superbly important men: Bashō, the haiku poet; Bankei, a Zen teacher; Hakuin, another Zen teacher; and Sengai, a Zen painter.

I want to say something about the work and genius of these four men, and the movement in Japanese history that they represent, which might be called the democratization of the esoteric. There is something about this idea that is of extraordinary interest to Americans, because, for better or worse, we live in a culture in which there is nothing esoteric. There are no secrets except those things that cannot be understood, which in a way are always esoteric. Only a few people can understand them; therefore, these secrets don't need to be guarded. If, for example, you publish a textbook on nuclear physics, in the sense that it is published, the subject ceases to be esoteric. Yet, it remains esoteric because so few people can understand it.

In our world, for example, teachers try their utmost to make themselves understood. They knock themselves out to make their message comprehensible without tears. But as I have explained, in Oriental cultures teachers expect the student to make the effort to attain the understanding. So, the teachers are difficult, and you must put yourself out to understand them. They are not going to make it easy for you, because of the belief that whatever comes to you too easily does not really come to you at all.

However, there was in seventeenth-century Japan a movement, among those people whom you might call esoteric, to make their understanding available to the masses. Remember the idea—arising out of Buddhist compassion—that the aim in life, of a Bodhisattva, is to bring enlightenment to as many other sentient beings as possible. And yet, the problem is that when you seek to popularize something, how do you do it without making it vulgar, cheap, watered down, insipid? These four men were in their own quite different ways geniuses at answering that question.

Let us start with Bashō. He did not invent haiku poetry, but he brought it to a degree of development whereby it was possible for ordinary people who were not very literate to become poets. To understand the situation in which Bashō arose, you must realize that Japanese poetry grows on the tree of Chinese tradition and that by the seventeenth century, Chinese poetry was as difficult to follow as, say, T. S. Eliot is today. To understand Eliot's *The Four Quartets,* you have to know an enormous amount of world literature and some very obscure books because it is a complex texture of allusions to other works. You have to know what these other works are in order to get the point. So this is poetry written strictly for literati. And the Chinese brought this to a high degree of perfection, until poets were writing only for other poets. They were not getting anything across to people who spoke only everyday language. And this happened also in Japan. If you read a novel like *The Tale of Genji,* you would read all about the light-footed amours of those very, very cultivated people, with their little poems and things, and the subtle kinds of allusions they made.

In the same way, the tea ceremony became overrefined, until there were suggestions in the shade of a cup that were intended to remind you of something, a complicated set of associations that the master had planned. People indulged in all kinds of fantastic one-upmanship, in seeing who did or did not recognize the subtle chains of association, recognition of which depended upon a great deal of learning. Well, you see that it is a very elaborate game. And the intent and the object of the game is not really delight but seeing who can out-associate whom. So these seventeenth-century masters rebelled against that kind of thing. They wanted tea and poetry and painting and Zen to be appreciated for themselves and to be appreciated by anybody with basic human equipment. So Bashō said that in order to write haiku, one should be taught by a child three feet high, because a statement that such a child would make would be a poem. And to the degree that what the child said was a simple image—just the kind of vivid statement that children often make—without philosophizing, it would be a profound poem.

"You light the fire, / and then I will show you something wonderful, / a great ball of snow." That is a haiku poem. Each of the following poems simply presents an image, and no more.

A brushwood gate, / and for a lock, / this snail.

Leaf fallen, / flying back to the branch, / butterfly.

You see there is something a little bit clever about those two, and for that very reason they are not the best kind of haiku. Better still is something like this:

"In the dense fog, / what is being shouted between / hill and boat."

You see the image of a river estuary hidden by fog, and you know there is someone down there in the boat talking to someone up on the hill, but you cannot make it out. You can't quite put your finger on it. That quality in Japanese aesthetics is called *yugen,* and it is made up of two Chinese characters, both of which mean "the dark, the deep, the mysterious." Yugen is not like a great abyss full of black clouds and lightning in which there might be a dragon, however. Yugen is the subtly mysterious, which the poet Seami said was like wandering on and on in a great forest without thought of return or watching flying geese appear and disappear in the clouds or watching distant fishing boats disappear behind islands.

Now, what in all these images is the connecting link? That is yugen.

We feel, from a Western standpoint, that haiku are unfinished. They are simply titles; first lines of something that could go on to elaborate and express everything. But in this kind of artistry, one leaves the best part unsaid, because the work of the poet is not to impress everybody with how clever he is, and leave them speechless, but to evoke something in the listener. In exactly the same way, the art of the painter—in the tradition of Sung Chinese painting—is to leave something to the beholder's imagination; hence, there is what is called "one-corner painting."

A painter like Mahiwon—or Byon, as he is known in Japanese—is a master of one-corner painting. He indicates a line of hills somewhere near the top, and down at the bottom there is a single drifting boat and a fisherman. This is all there is. The path, as it were, comes to an end in the parsley. To understand this, you have to go back to childhood. Remember how as a child you loved to explore paths and get right down among the stalks of grasses and weeds, to see where it all goes? One of the eternal children's stories is that you were one day walking along a little lane and discovered a door in a wall that you had never seen before. You opened it, and it led into a magical garden where all the bushes were covered in jewels, and there were marvelous birds and fantastic songs. And you came out because you had to get home in time for dinner, and the next day you looked for that door again but you couldn't find it anywhere. You knew it was there—it was just between this fence and that fence. But today it isn't there. And yet somehow it is always there.

So, for every child there is always a kind of funny place that leads to somewhere else, and you don't figure out exactly where it leads because that would spoil it. You mustn't know. And all this haiku poetry, and this kind of painting that the Sung artists so marvelously mastered, seeks to evoke that sense of what I would call possibility or potentiality, without actually filling in any details. And that is real magic. This is the way to suggest the abysmally evil, and it is likewise the way to suggest the ineffably beautiful. Do not fill in the details. Indicate; do not explain.

Let us take some other examples. Consider the famous Ryoan-ji Garden in Japan. The most important thing about Japanese gardens is the background in which you find them. You cannot take Ryoan-ji, as people have attempted to do, and reconstruct it in Brooklyn unless you reconstruct the background, too, and that is going to be pretty difficult to do. Now what is that background? There is a wall along the back of the garden, a rather low wall, but just high enough because it lies on the crest of a slope. Beyond it the hill descends. All you see beyond the wall is trees. So, too, in many of the gardens around the temples in Japan, you will see over the wall perhaps a roof, and then beyond that, treetops. And those treetops, although the temple is in the middle of a dense city, somehow suggest that outside the garden is a forest.

There is something else. You know the quality of sky as you see it over the tops of the hills that lie between you and the ocean: there is something very distant in the blue of that sky, suggesting miles and miles and miles of space, and gulls and pelicans drifting away into the distance. Openness. Something that, in other words, your spirit goes out into and has nowhere to land. Now, that kind of quality is yugen. And the trick in haiku is to evoke the mood of yugen, a certain sort of mysterious suggestiveness, by very simple means that do not actually pin anything down. That is the point of haiku poetry, to put this possibility within the reach of people who had within themselves the capability, the sensitivity, to appreciate the yugen feeling or another feeling that is called *sabi*. Sabi is akin to yugen. It refers to a certain kind of solitariness or loneliness, good loneliness—not the loneliness that plucks at the heart strings and makes you long for friends. That is not sabi. Sabi is when you love to be alone and are at peace in this loneliness.

There is also another mood, but still akin to these two, which in Japanese is called *aware*. It is spelled like our word *aware* only pronounced "a-war-e." And this, like yugen and sabi, is difficult to translate. It is a sense of sadness, but delightful sadness.

There is a poem which says, "Even in the mind of a no-mind man, there is *aware* when the snipe leaves the marsh on an autumn evening." Think of late autumn, when all nature is foggy and cold and the leaves have almost gone, and the last sign of life—the bird, the snipe—leaves and goes somewhere else, perhaps farther south, when the last geese have migrated and winter has set in. It is to say that even in the mind of a no-mind mind—that is to say, in the mind of a buddha, who has no egocentric feelings—even in the mind of such a person, there comes a clutch of sadness. *Aware* is a sort of nostalgia, and we feel it very strongly in all the poetry of transience. This is one of the greatest themes of poetry. The world is floating away. Nothing can be possessed. We are all dissolving smoke. Poets keep on about this, and so do preachers, but in different ways. The preacher says, "Vanity of vanities, all is vanity." But in the next moment he will burst into poetry. That chapter in Ecclesiastes, where everything is described as passing away— how exquisite it is. The same magic is evoked in Shakespeare:

Our revels now are ended. These our actors,
As I foretold you, were all spirits and
Are melted into air, into thin air:
And, like the baseless fabric of this vision,
The cloud-capp'd towers, the gorgeous palaces,
The solemn temples, the great globe itself,
Yea, all which it inherit shall dissolve
And, like this insubstantial pageant faded,
Leave not a rack behind. We are such stuff
As dreams are made on, and our little life
Is rounded with a sleep.

What is going on here? From one point of view, the poet seems to be putting everything down, to be saying that all is a vision, all is an illusion. And yet at the same time the poet borrows from this vision. He borrows the beautiful imagery of cloud-capped towers, gorgeous palaces, and solemn temples. And from the illusion itself he weaves his spell.

Fitzgerald's *Omar Khayyám* seems a bit corny to us now, to ears trained by modern poetry, but to the Victorian ear it had the same magic. "The earthly hope men set their hearts upon turns ashes, or it prospers, and anon like a snow upon the desert's dusty face, lighting a little hour or two, is gone."

Oriental poetry—haiku, every kind of Buddhist sutra—is full of the theme of the disappearing world, the floating world that vanishes.

Now one kind of person would say, "Uh-uh-uh, no, don't you look at those beautiful girls, because in a few years they're going to be ugly old ladies. Don't take delight in this delicious food, because in a few years you are going to have chronic stomach ulcers and bad digestion. Don't dissipate yourself with singing and dancing, because not long from now you will have rheumatism or arthritis, and a sore throat, and you won't be able to enjoy it anymore."

But another kind of person would say, "Yup, it all dissolves. It all goes away. The beautiful girls will become old ladies, the handsome young men will become crones, and eventually they will all become bare skulls. And isn't that great?"

What is wrong with skeletons? When you pick up a seashell on the beach, you say, "No one home anymore. All the flesh in this bone is dissolved." And you say, "Wow, look at that. Isn't that great?"

A skull is just as beautiful as a seashell. It is a bone that a brain once lived in; a bone from which jeweled eyes once shown. But still, look at that white skull—it is really a marvelous thing. We have been taught wrong associations. We have been taught that the going-away of life is against life, but as a matter of fact, life is entirely something that always goes away. Going away—dissolving—is the same thing as living. But if we are taught that dying is against life, then we can't live. Dying is the same thing as living. Everything becomes bones; everything turns back into the soil, becomes fertilizer. That is life. A loved one must be allowed to dissolve and not be clung to. So this is why the seam of transience and dissolution is really one of the mainstays of poetic beauty. And the poet is a genius, and a compassionate Bodhisattva to us all, when he takes the thing that we dread—that is to dissolve—and shows us that such dissolution is the heart of beauty and the heart of life. That beauty is what the mood of *aware* in haiku and painting and poetry seeks to evoke.

Now, I have gotten a rather long way away from the other three gentlemen I started to talk about, so let's move on to Sengi. Sengi was a Zen master who made the greatest thing out of marvelously bad paintings. In a way, you might say of Sengi that he couldn't paint. Nor could he write. His writing is like a child's, and his paintings are caricatures. And yet they are not. There is something about him that is extremely humorous. He enjoyed, always, a joke on himself—about how badly he wrote, how badly he painted, and the fact that he got away with it. In fact, he became so famous in the seventeenth century that people started to copy him, thinking it was a cinch to do what he did—that anybody could paint like Sengi. In the same way, some people look at a modern abstract painting and say, "Well, my child could do better than that."

There was one painter in Kyoto who was making quite a lot of money forging Sengi paintings and selling them. And one day Sengi came to visit him, and he said to this man, "I have brought you my seals. Your forgeries of my paintings are so good that if you would actually put my own seals on them, they would be perfect.

"But," he said, "excuse me if I borrow them occasionally, because I might need them myself."

Now, what is Sengi doing? He is a man who has been greatly collected but who painted for the joy of painting, not to be shown. That is to say, he had no ambitions to be hung in a gallery or a museum. He just liked to draw. So he is trying to say that in order to be a painter, you don't have to be shown in a gallery. And that if you paint to be shown in a gallery, you are not going to be a genuine painter.

Has it ever occurred to you that people who want to be

shown in museums, who have that as their supreme ambition in painting, are doing a very odd thing? A museum is a kind of morgue. Real artists paint to have their paintings lived with or put in a house; they paint a screen that is actually going to be used as a piece of furniture in a room. Painting, in other words, is something as useful in its own way as plumbing. It makes a gorgeous house. It isn't made just to be shown, to be a fad, to be talked about, to have art historians going *cluck, cluck, cluck*. The moment it becomes that, it becomes the same kind of thing as poetry that cannot be understood unless you know the allusions. It becomes academic painting.

So Sengi restores painting to seventeenth-century art as something to be done not to be a fake little gallery artist but to thoroughly enjoy yourself with a brush.

So it is with Zen. Zen, too, can become too clerical. And so it does, with professional Zen. I was discussing this with a good Western Zen student once, and she said, "Do you know, if you stay around a teacher too long, he starts to get worried about you. That is to say, if you are not going to be a teacher yourself, if you are not going to be a priest, if you're just a lay student of Zen, and if you go back to this guy year after year after year, he starts to get troubled and says that you're addicted, that it's becoming a bad habit. That somehow you have to get rid of Zen. Wherever these things become professional, people lose their spirit."

And so there emerged these two other men in the seventeenth century who in quite different ways helped make it possible for Zen understanding to spread beyond a sort of clerical circle. Hakuin did it by one method, and Banke by another. And very interesting results arose from this. Hakuin was an extraordinarily clever teacher. He systematized the koan system in such a way that it could be very conveniently handled, and he had eighty students who became accomplished Zen masters. That was considered absolutely extraordinary because, before Hakuin, it had been felt that one Zen master would have only one or two really good students, who would become his spiritual descendants. It was felt that in this present age of the Kali yuga—when everything is falling apart—you could not possibly expect more than that. So Hakuin, by his very ingenious but rigorous discipline, was a martinet. He really was. But he encouraged many young Japanese to go through the mill of his technique. And somehow, by pepping them up and challenging them with vigorous discipline, he allowed eighty students to succeed him.

Now Banke did exactly the opposite. He taught Zen mainly to farmers. He was the roshi at a temple in Kyoto for many years, and he taught to the simplest people. He said that to understand Zen, you didn't really have to do anything; that if you try to attain satori, it's like trying to wash blood off with blood. What you have to understand is your unborn mind. This idea is hard to put into English. You have to understand the nonmanifest, which hasn't yet arisen into the world of appearances. He said, "Because of your unborn mind, when you hear a crow squawk or when you hear a bell ring, you know instantly, without any premeditation or without having to stop to think, what has happened."

One day there was a Nishirin priest heckling Banke out in the back of the audience, saying, "I don't understand what you're talking about." Nishirin shu is a very belligerent form of Buddhism—it is like Jehovah's Witnesses in Buddhism. So Banke said, "I would be happy to explain, please come closer." And the Nishirin priest came closer, and Banke said, "Come closer still." And the Nishirin priest kept on coming. When he was right up there with Banke, Banke said, "How well you understand me."

So Banke would say, "Zen consists in faith in your innate quality of intelligence, in your organic pattern. Trust it. After all, your eyes are beautifully blue or brown, your hair is wonderfully brunette or blond. Your breathing is fantastic. Your heart is working beautifully. That is your Zen. Go ahead." And all those farmers, and the other people who came around, understood Banke. But Banke didn't leave any disciples. He had no spiritual successors. And for this reason he is considered, in a certain way, an enormous success, because he was like a bird going through the sky without leaving any traces. As the poem says,

"Entering the water, he does not make a ripple. / Entering the forest, he does not disturb a blade of grass."

Banke is largely forgotten today because of this. Those who are remembered, you see, are those who left spiritual descendants who could show a certificate and say, "See, I was trained by such and such a master, who was trained by such a master, who was trained by such a master." In all such genealogies, however, there is a temptation toward formalism and a certain kind of pride. So, in a sense, by leaving no specific descendants, he at the same time left many nameless descendants, people who were totally unimportant historically, who were farmers and peasants, but who really got the point of what he said. They decided, then and there, that because they understood, there was no need to become professional Zen Buddhists. They understood that there was no need to label themselves as Banke followers or Zen followers or Buddhists, because whoever really gets this thing and understands it knows that he hasn't attained anything.

In the *Diamond Sutra* Buddha said, "When I attained complete perfect and unexcelled awakening, I attained nothing at all." And you see that nothing at all is the same nothing into which all trees and plants and bodies and butterflies and birds are disappearing in the course of endless transformations. Everything disappears into nothing at all, but out of that same nothing at all come all the new things, forever and ever.

CHAPTER SIX

Return to the Forest

During the past few months I have been studying an extraordinarily interesting paper written by Joseph Campbell, whose name will be familiar to many of you as the author of a book on mythology called *The Hero with a Thousand Faces*. Joseph Campbell is also the editor of the posthumous works of Heinrich Zimmer, which have been published by the Bollingen Foundation. As a matter of fact, many of those works are his own original writings, since they were compiled from Henrich Zimmer's notes. But the paper I am referring to was presented I think in 1957, in August, at the Eranos Conference in Switzerland, at a meeting of scholars and philosophers and psychologists and scientists who gather every year under the auspices of a woman who has for a long time been interested in the work of C. G. Jung. The particular paper that Joseph Campbell presented at this conference is called *The Symbol Without Meaning* and is an exploration of an extraordinary phenomenon in the history of religions—which you might call the development and the dissolution of cosmologies, of great views of the world, under religio-philosophical auspices—which is the language about the universe that has been devised by various cultures. Now, Campbell distinguishes two great phases in man's religious history. He equates them with two styles of culture, which predate our own technological style of culture. These are the hunting cultures and the agrarian cultures. He points out that the kind of religion characteristic of a hunting culture is what generally goes by the name of shamanism, although that particular word is distinctive of Mongolian styles of so-called primitive religion. Nevertheless, the phenomenon known as shamanism is found distributed all over the planet. Shamanism is characteristically a very individualistic type of religiousness. That is to say, the religious experience of the shaman is not something that he gets from an authoritative priesthood. It is not something handed down from generation to generation, which he goes to a human teacher to learn. The shaman is a solitary medicine man, a man of power, who invariably has to find his experience for himself. Usually it is by going alone into the dangerous forest and undergoing some kind of ordeal, not necessarily on the physical level but always in the psychic world, the world of spirits.

When he comes through the ordeal, he comes out an initiate of power. The reason one must attach so much importance to the individual character of this experience is that it goes along with the general style of a hunting culture, in which every individual man contains the whole culture. That is to say, it is not the kind of culture in which there is a division of labor. The hunter spends much of his time on his own. He has to learn to take care of himself in the forests, without any other human aid. And although hunting cultures have societies and social groups, they are composed of men with their women and children, men who are equals because of the type of life that they follow.

Now, an entirely different state of affairs arises within a settled agrarian culture. Here, because the style of life is more complex, a division of labor is required. You begin to see not only a separation of human beings into various castes and various functions but also the necessity of devising far more complex language and institutions to provide communication between them. And this always involves a very, very powerful socialization of the individual. Spending his time more and more in a settled place, he therefore has greater intercourse with other people. He has to learn to think in accordance with common patterns, whether these patterns be based on language, on the type of work, or on the geographical features of the area that he inhabits. Each individual has to subordinate himself to a socially implanted view of life, because only under these conditions is communication between individuals possible. And so it comes about that the style of religiousness that one associates with an agrarian, as distinct from a hunting, culture is a traditional and authoritative style of religion in which the individual derives his experience from a tradition usually embodied in a priesthood. And Campbell goes on to point out that the first historical instances of the appearance of the familiar circle symbol, which is called in Sanskrit the *mandala*, are associated with the agrarian cultures. No example of this kind of symbol is found archaeologically prior to the development of an agrarian community.

Now, I might say something about the mandala as a mythological, world-symbol, although anybody who has studied the works of C. G. Jung is already very familiar with it. A mandala is essentially a circle, usually divided into four quarters, or into multiples of four, and embodies, as it were, the general theme of the integration of a community. It is not unlike, for example, a stockaded village or city, with a ring of defense around a center. Campbell shows that the symbol represents the kind of society in which functions are divided among specialists. We find that in many of these ancient societies the functions are divided precisely into four groups, just as they are in medieval European society. We have the spiritual power, the priesthood; the temporal power, the nobility; the commoners; and the serfs. In ancient Indian society we have the Brahman caste, the priesthood; the Kshatriya caste, the rulers and soldiers; the Vaisya caste, the commons or merchants; and the Sudra caste, the laborers. These four castes, represented by the four divisions of the mandala, together form the common, integrated, encircled community. And the important point that Campbell makes about its religiousness is that it was carried down by tradition, by an authoritative priestly caste, and was experienced altogether by the community. The whole style of life in a community of this kind depended upon communication, and we can communicate with one another not only by virtue of a shared, common language but also, and more important, by virtue of a shared, common view of the world. Of course, this is why those who have the private type of sensuous experiences we call hallucinations and illusions do not fit easily into a community. But Campbell's paper goes on to show that every so often social cosmologies and other views of the world held in common by societies tend to break up. He actually begins his paper with a reference to the fifteenth century, when because of the expansion of the Western world through the exploration of the surface of the globe, as well as a greater knowledge of astronomy, the geocentric view of the Ptolomeic universe—the view of the world under which Christianity itself had come to birth—began to break up. And this he looks upon as a breaking up of the mandala, the communal, agreed-upon, stable picture of the world, by means of which people were able to communicate with one another. It was a breaking up, therefore, that involved a disruption of all means of communication, and the throwing of culture into a fundamental confusion.

It is perhaps just because of this breaking up of a unified worldview, and a subsequent entry into the confused, relativistic world of modern thought, that Western peoples have become interested in other, earlier attempts to deal with life as it must be lived during times when the mandala, as it were, was breaking up. For after all, the idea of going beyond a communal view of the world, and somehow managing to get along without that world, is not a new thing. It is very interesting that in ancient Indian society—and to some extent even still, in modern Indian society—when a man has done his work in society and is able to hand over his caste duties to his son, or sons, he abandons the world, as it were, and gives up caste, becoming what is ordinarily called a *sunyasan*. We think that that word usually means "holy man" or "hermit" or "spiritual devotee." But what is of particular interest, in connection with our current discussion, is that the abandonment of caste is also thought of as entering into the state of *vanaprastha*. Now, *vanaprastha* means a "forest dweller." The man who gives up caste goes to the style of life that predates the agrarian culture. He goes back, as it were, to shamanism.

And this is true not only in the Indian culture but also in the Chinese. The Confucian way of life represents the community of convention, which is what the mandala also corresponds to: the nice, enclosed, tight little world in which we can feel we understand one another and our environment. It is the Taoist philosophy, by contrast, that corresponds to the Indian search for liberation, or *moksha*, that is to say, to liberation from the socially conditioned view of the world.

There is evidence to show that the solitary, Taoist sage has some sort of ancestral connection with the shaman. And it is also possible that the words *shamana* in Sanskrit and *shaman* in Chinese both have their origin in the term *shaman*. The shamana is the man who has given up social life in the world. Likewise, the shaman in Chinese is the lonely sage in quest of immortality who has gone by himself into the mountains and the forests.

Of course, we should not suppose that the entry into the stage of vanaprastha, or the Taoist sage's return to the forest, is in the strict sense of the word, a regression. It's no more a regression than is the wise man's becoming again as a child a regression. We don't mean that he has literally become childish, that he has forgotten how to think and speak and behave in human society. Neither does the person who enters into the stage of vanaprastha become a wolf man or a wild savage who runs around in the jungle naked and eats his food off the ground with his teeth. He does not do anything of the kind. But there is some sort of analogy between vanaprastha and going back to the shaman's religion, or to the life of the hunter. At the same time, it also refers to going beyond the place we find ourselves in society, where the worldview is a conditioned social pattern.

Now, in what sense, in just what way, is vanaprastha a going beyond society? And how does it apply to our own situation? We are not, as it were, voluntarily going beyond our own nice, clear, authoritative, comfortable view of the world. We are rather being forced beyond it by the pressure of events, the uncertainty of our times, and the confusion and instability of modern thought, which separate us from a secure and humanly comfortable picture of the universe.

Well, first of all, it must be obvious that one of the things principally involved by a social system of communication is that it is a form of what Korjipsky has called "time binding." The whole possibility of thought and language involves a codification of experience. It involves a form of thinking about life that is, after all, basically description. Now, description is a way of coding, of putting into symbols the events that go by us. And as we begin to be able to put events into symbols, we develop most peculiar powers of memory. It becomes much easier to recollect and to formalize what has happened to us. And along with this, naturally, comes the ability to project our recollection into thoughts about the future. And this, apparently, is something that very primitive types of human beings do not do to any great extent. But for our ability to describe and to prefigure what is going to happen, we pay a very alarming price. By being able to think about all sorts of future possibilities we are able to experience the emotions appropriate to those possibilities as if they were present happenings. In other words, civilized man tends to be in a state of chronic worry and fear and anxiety, because he is always confronted not with the simple actuality of what is happening before him but with the innumerable possibilities of what might happen. And since, because of this, his emotional existence tends to be in a chronic state of anxiety and tension, he increasingly loses the ability to relate to the concrete world as it manifests itself to him in the actual present in which he lives. He becomes so tied up inside that, as it were, the channels of his sensibility become blocked. He gets a kind of neurological sclerosis, a kind of inability to give himself permission to be spontaneous, to be alive with full joyous abandonment. Thus, the more civilized we become, the more stuffy we get. And, therefore, the need arises for various ways of liberating ourselves from society, for entering what the Indians call vanaprastha, the life of a forest dweller. Because when a person reaches a certain point in life when he says, "I have had enough of all this. I am simply tired of making life not worth living, by constantly living through the horrors of what might happen, for the sake of efficiency and membership in the community. Let me just get away from it all for a while and find out what the score is for me, myself. I am tired of being told what I ought to believe. I am tired of being told how I ought to see, how I ought to behave, how I ought to feel. Let me find out for myself who I really am." And so, these institutions that allow one to go

back, as it were, to the shaman state of religion, to get away
from the community interpretation of how one ought to think
and feel, have arisen in a great many cultures. And they are
arising again today.

It is impossible and misleading to pretend to have what I
would call an authoritative attitude about this phase of man's
spiritual exploration. Sometimes, for example, when a person
wants to find out who he really is, and he goes to a psychiatrist,
he will occasionally find the kind who does not have an authoritative view of what human health is and who simply helps the
individual to find his own way. Other times, unfortunately, he
will find a doctrinaire psychotherapist who thinks he knows
what an integrated, healthy, normal human being is; who has
rigid, theoretic beliefs about what the actual facts of human
nature are, the actual design of the psyche; and who attempts,
consciously or subconsciously, to wangle the patient into
accepting his views.

Similarly, we may get from the Orient, from books or
authorities, information about ways of liberation, which have
hardened into an orthodoxy and which present these ways of
liberation just exactly as if they were the kinds of spiritual experiences that it is the function of that social officer, the priest, to
impart. And thus, when we get swamis representing an
orthodox interpretation of Indian moksha, or liberation, or even
when we get Zen masters representing an orthodox Buddhist

experience, we should be suspicious because these are the kind of experiences that cannot be transmitted and that, because of their very nature, are things that one must find out for oneself. And if they could be explained, if they could be transmitted, they would therefore fail to be the very things they are intended to be, because they are discoveries of something authentic, of something genuine and firsthand between oneself and one's universe. And, thus, it is in the nature of things that they cannot be codified; they cannot be made a factor in social communication.

And so, it is in a way fortunate that we in the Western world do not have too many authoritative masters and teachers to whom we feel we can now go for enlightenment. More and more of us, I think, tend to feel that we are all alone together, whistling in the dark, that we haven't a savior. There is no statesman clever enough to understand the frightful tangle of international affairs or to really do anything much about them. There is no psychologist or physician or philosopher who really impresses us as having the last word on everything. More and more, each one of us is thrown on our own resources. And this seems to me to be a perfectly excellent state of affairs. We have, in a symbolic sense, come back to the forest, like the hunter of old, who had nobody around him to tell him how he ought to feel and how he ought to use his senses, who was required, therefore, to make his own exploration of the world and to discover it for himself.

But as you learn when you study the records of these self-discoveries, the fascinating thing about them is that there is so much agreement among all those who do discover the world for themselves.

And yet, you do not achieve this agreement by seeking it. It is not achieved by looking out of the corner of your eye to see if everybody else is getting the same results as you or by trying to find out what others have already discovered. It is achieved by going down into one's own inner, secret place and asking there for a direct encounter with the world, independent of convention.

It is in this way that a person becomes, in the truest sense of the word, a self—an original, authoritative source of life—as distinct from being simply a person in the original sense of *persona*: a mask, a role to be played in society.